STO

ACPL ITEM

S0-DSF-874

621
WIL
CHILTON'S GUIDE TO MACINTOSH
REPAIR AND MAINTENANCE

DISCARDED

3 1833 01918 6870

621.3916 W67c
WILLIAMS, GENE B.
CHILTON'S GUIDE TO MACINTOSH
REPAIR AND MAINTENANCE

ALLEN COUNTY PUBLIC LIBRARY
FORT WAYNE, INDIANA 46802

You may return this book to any agency, branch,
or bookmobile of the Allen County Public Library.

CHILTON'S Guide
to
Macintosh
Repair and Maintenance

Gene B. Williams

Chilton Book Company
Radnor, Pennsylvania

Allen County Public Library
Ft. Wayne, Indiana

Copyright © 1986 by Gene B. Williams
All Rights Reserved
Published in Radnor, Pennsylvania 19089 by Chilton Book Company

No part of this book may be reproduced, transmitted or stored
in any form or by any means, electronic or mechanical,
without prior written permission from the publisher

Manufactured in the United States of America

Library of Congress Cataloging in Publication Data
Williams, Gene B.
    Chilton's guide to Macintosh repair and maintenance.
    Includes index.
    1. Microcomputers—Maintenance and repair.
2. Macintosh (Computer) I. Title
TK7887.W535   1986   621.391'6   85-48271
ISBN 0-8019-7639-1 (pbk.)

1 2 3 4 5 6 7 8 9 0   5 4 3 2 1 0 9 8 7 6

To Danny:
Welcome to our world

Contents

Preface

A few years ago I bought my first computer. I was facing a tight deadline. The salesperson had inspected the computer before I packed it into my car and brought it to the office. Back in the office, it was plugged in, booted up with the program. Nothing! The screen was blank.

I called the seller to explain the problem. He said that he couldn't be out until the following Wednesday. So much for my deadline. The only solution was to try a diagnosis by phone.

He told me to open the case. I was convinced that the second I did that, the machine would be ruined for all time. A look inside confirmed my fears. There were what seemed to be several hundred memory boards along with enough mysterious components to launch the next deep space probe. I had about as much desire to touch the insides of the machine as I have to jump out of a moving car.

Under the dealer's direction, each board was pulled, cleaned, and inserted back into the system board. What should have been a 30-second job took 30 minutes. I was so sure that every movement would break something important that I did everything *very* slowly.

I tried to get the computer to operate again, thinking that a reset might cure the trouble. Absolutely nothing! The dealer repeated, "I really can't make it there before Wednesday. Oh, by the way, have you checked the contrast control? Maybe you bumped it."

"Contrast control? What contrast control?"

"It's on the left, beneath the keyboard."

I reached under and felt a little wheel. "You mean that little wheel thingy?"

Suddenly the screen came to life with all the signs and symbols it was supposed to display. The problem was solved and I met the deadline.

As the months went by I ran into other problems. Each time I went through the same feelings of helplessness. A computer is such a complicated piece of machinery, isn't it? Doesn't a person need years of training and experience, plus a room full of special tools and test equipment, to repair one?

Most of my problems turned out to be minor. I was able to handle most repairs with tools no more complex than a screwdriver. A few times I had to get "technical" and use an ordinary voltmeter.

Then I became involved with other computers. The knowledge I'd gained with my first computer carried over. From conversations with other computer owners, it became obvious that most people not only knew very little about their machines but were also nearly terrified of them.

As a result, this series of repair and maintenance handbooks was developed. Each is written for the typical end user—the person with no technical training or background. They will help you in taking care of the most common failures in a personal computer system. With rare exception, you *can* do it. A computer is nothing all that grand and mysterious. It's just a machine. Sophisticated perhaps, but a machine all the same, and less complicated than you might think.

There are only so many reasons a machine fails to work. Most can be quickly and easily spotted by almost anyone, given a few tips and guidelines. Fancy equipment and technical degrees are not needed in most cases; a bit of common sense—and this book—are enough.

If you're standing in a bookstore reading this, be aware that the goal of this book is to save you *at least* ten times its cost. More important to some, the savings aren't just monetary. You will save a great deal of time, both in waiting for the technician and in driving to and from the shop. BUY IT! If you've already bought this book, congratulations! You won't regret it.

Apple offers several models. The II Series models (II, II+, IIe, and IIc) are covered in *How to Repair and Maintain Your Apple Computer*, also in Chilton's Business Computing series. This book provides information on the Macintosh alone; it covers many of the common configurations of the Macintosh system, plus possible modifications, including the MacCharlie IBM PC emulation package.

My thanks to several people who were helpful in putting this book together: At the top of the list is Greg Guerin, my technical advisor for this book (and, I hope, for more to come). Stacy Farmer, John Duhring, and all the people at Apple were of great help in providing technical support as the book was being researched and assembled. Invaluable assistance was given by Larry Wilson of Mesa Computer Mart. Then there are those, such as Chris Mitchell and Deke Barker, who read each book in the series for ease of understanding.

Introduction

Not all that many years ago, the world of computing was more or less confined to big business. The average person couldn't hope to afford a computer. Special schooling was needed just to operate one. Then along came the remarkable idea that computing need not be difficult or mysterious, followed immediately by the advent of home computers.

The popularity of home computers is due largely to the fact that they are becoming easier and easier to operate. When the first home computers were introduced, the person who had one was thought of as a genius (or a "nut"). There were very few commercial programs available, which meant that the owner of a home computer had to have a solid knowledge of programming to do anything at all. All that has changed.

Ask any ten people today. Several will own a computer. More yet will be thinking about it. Nine out of ten are likely to have some kind of computer around—a pocket calculator if nothing else.

Almost anyone can operate a computer. You might enjoy your computer more if you learn some programming, but all you really need are preprogrammed diskettes. Push one in, press a few keys, and you're ready to go.

Meanwhile, the cost for technical work such as repair and installation of add-ons has jumped. Charges of $60 or more per hour for labor alone are common. Some shops charge a $150 minimum just for looking at a malfunctioning machine. If the technician comes to your home or place of business, all costs increase.

Average downtime for such a repair is three days. Having the machine tied up for a week or more isn't unusual.

To avoid these high costs and inconveniences, some owners purchase a repair contract. Typical yearly cost is between 5% and 10% of the purchase price. A fee of 20% isn't unheard of. Several sources list a monthly cost of 1% of the system purchase price as the minimum repair costs to be expected without such a contract.

To make things even more depressing (but more heartening for readers of this book), it has been said that 95% of all repairs and other technical work could be taken care of by the computer owner without special tools or technical background. Strange as it might sound, at least half of all "repairs" aren't repairs at all and require no tools. Another third will require nothing more complicated than your fingers. When tools *are* needed, it's rare that you'll need anything but simple, ordinary tools you probably have already. (See "Tools You'll Need" at the end of this chapter.) There is often no need for you to spend hundreds of dollars, to wait a week or even a day while the repair is being done, or to waste time going to and from the shop.

ADVANTAGES OF THIS BOOK

The purpose of this book is to show you just how easy it is to diagnose and repair most malfunctions. It will also show you how easy it is to maintain a system to reduce repairs. You don't need a knowledge of electronics. It helps, but you can handle many repairs without it.

Chapter 1 acquaints you with the rules of the game. Its purpose is to show you what can cause trouble or damage, both to you and to the computer. Dangerous spots are revealed to prevent you from getting a shock. Cautions and precautions are given to keep you from making costly mistakes. Read this chapter thoroughly and put the information to use and you are highly unlikely to run into trouble while working on your computer.

Chapter 2 shows you how to diagnose malfunctions and how to get your computer to diagnose itself. This chapter provides tips on how to track a problem. Chapters 3, 4, 5, and 6 take you deeper into the specific problem areas.

Proper maintenance can reduce repair costs dramatically. Chapter 7 tells you how to reduce problems and repair costs by prevention. After you've read this chapter you'll know what to do and what not to do. Knowing how to do many of the little tasks to keep your computer happy and healthy can save you a great deal of time, expense, and frustration.

The Macintosh was designed by Apple to be a complete system right out of the box. Still, additions or changes can be made. Unless you know ahead of time exactly what you need in a computer system (in which case, you're a rare individual), there will come a time when you want to add something to your computer. It might be a second printer, a phone modem, or some modification to the hardware to make the computer more versatile. Whatever you care to add, you'll find the help you need in Chapter 8.

By following the steps in Chapter 2, you'll have a good idea of what the malfunction is and whether or not you handle the job yourself. This knowledge helps reduce repair costs and greatly decreases the risk of being ripped off by unnecessary repairs. Chapter 9 gives you some tips on what to look for in a technician and how to deal with this person.

Even if you have no background in electronics, you can still handle most repairs and maintenance. However, the more you know, the easier it will be. Check with your local library for books on basic and advanced electronics. The less knowledge of electronics you have, the more important it becomes that you pick up such books. Your goal is not to become an electronics whiz, just to have a more thorough understanding of what is going wrong inside your computer and why.

It is suggested that you read the entire book before attempting any repairs. Even those sections you don't think you'll need are important, because they will help give you an overall picture of the workings of your computer. Don't be in so much of a hurry that you end up causing more problems.

Before you start yanking out parts or devices, go through Chapter 2 (diagnosis) carefully. Imagine that something has gone wrong and the computer will not accept programs. Proper diagnosis will guide you to the source of the malfunction. If the problem is with the drives, why spend time with the printer? The few minutes you spend with this chapter can save you hours of wasted effort.

Once you're familiar with Chapter 2, you can go to the appropriate chapter for further details. For example, if diagnosis indicates that the problem is with the disk drive, turn to Chapter 4. If the problem seems to be with the power supply, go to Chapter 6.

Use this book correctly and it should save you at least ten times its cost in the first repair. (As a practical example, my own system board failed. By using the information in Chapter 5, I saved close to $200.) Instead of spending that 1% per month ($420 per year on a $3500 system) or that 10% per year ($350 on the $3500 system), you could be spending only $50 per year, or much less.

Why spend more than you have to?

Expenses aren't in money alone. The time involved may be quite costly: time spent waiting for the technician to come or time wasted in driving to and from the shop. Then there is downtime, when your valuable computer is useless.

You bought your computer to save time. Why use up what you've saved in waiting hours or days only to find that you could have fixed the trouble yourself in a few seconds?

An added benefit will be that you will understand your system better. You'll know what can go wrong. You'll learn how to fix the most common problems, and even how to prevent troubles.

Note

If the computer or peripheral is still under warranty, DO NOT attempt to open the cabinet. This will void the warranty. Bring the suspected device to an authorized dealer.

TOOLS YOU'LL NEED

The Macintosh is a highly sophisticated and well-designed machine. However, it is not like previous computers made by Apple. Apple designed it to discourage the end user from opening the main cabinet. A special screwdriver is needed to get the screws out. The head of this screw, called a Torx head (Fig. i-1), is a like a six-pointed star. It cannot be safely removed with a regular or Phillips screwdriver. A Torx screwdriver is needed.

For most of the screws, a standard Torx screwdriver, T-15 in size, will do the job. There are two screws under the handle, however, that require a longer reach—about an inch or so longer than the standard size. A minimum of an 8-inch-long shaft is needed to reach under the molded handle to remove those two screws.

Finding this special tool can be difficult, although it will become easier

Torx-head Screw
top view

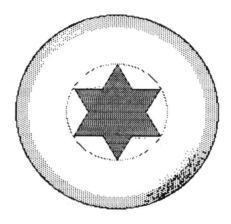

FIG. I—1 Torx head screwdriver.

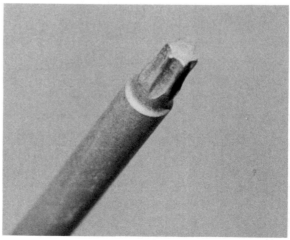

FIG. I—2 Torx driver.

as this new screw head becomes more popular. By the time this book is released, it may be possible to find not only the longer-bladed tools, but extension tips for rachet drivers as well.

If you can't find one in your area, you can make one fairly easily. You even have two choices as to how you go about it.

The first step either way is to buy a T-15 Torx driver and cut the tip and some of the blade from the handle with a hack saw. For safety, use a file to clean the sharp edges made by the cutting and remove all burrs. What you have left is the tip and blade by itself, and a handle.

You can now insert the blade into the end of a screwdriving tool that takes bits. (You may have to file the cut end of the blade into a square or hex to fit.)

If you don't have one of these drivers around already, it might be cheaper (and easier) to bring the job to a local machine shop or welder. They have the proper tools and equipment for making such modifications, and for them it's not a major job. You can get your own customized Torx driver made for just a few dollars. (Dig out the phone book and call around. Machine shops will probably be able to do the job. Welding shops might be able to do it faster and cheaper, depending on where you live.)

The end result doesn't have to be pretty—just functional. Even if the shop does nothing more than weld a small insert into the middle of the length of the blade (about an inch of metal, and two welded joints), it will do the trick.

Another special tool is needed to get into the cabinet. Even after all the screws are removed, the case will still be stuck together. Some people try to unsnap the two parts by prying with a screwdriver. Damage is almost guaranteed if you try this. Others try to yank the cover apart with sheer physical force, which is better but could also be an invitation for disaster.

The official Apple repair shops use a tool called a case popper (Fig. i-3). This tool looks something like two large putty knives hooked together with handles and springs. These wide blades spread the force and help prevent damage to the plastic cabinet.

You can attempt to build such a tool. Some people have limited success by using two putty knives with a screwdriver handle as a fulcrum between the two. Once again, this is an inexpensive method of prying apart the cabinet, but it is risky.

A little better is to adapt a brass hinge for this purpose. The hinge blades will help to spread the force. By screwing the hinge to wood handles, you should be able to apply that force evenly.

If the local Apple store can't (or won't) sell the tool to you, and you lack the skills, perhaps you can get a local machine shop to build something suitable for you.

There are some basic tips to keep in mind when you separate the cover. First, since you are prying apart soft plastic, you want to spread the force over as much area as possible. Second, the edges of the tool should be

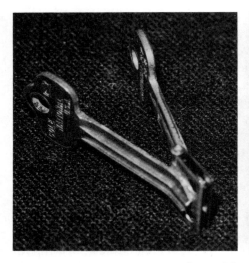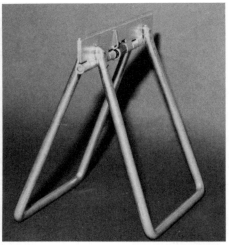

FIG. I–3 The case popper (right) and homemade version (left; see Appendix A).

smooth, not sharp, to reduce any possibility of gouging. Third, the two parts must move apart in as straight a motion as you can manage. Any angle can cause additional damage. Fourth, even if you have the official case popper, start on the bottom. The first separation is the worst, and the most prone to cause damage to the case. If it happens on the bottom, that damage won't show.

FIG. I–4 The inside of the Macintosh.

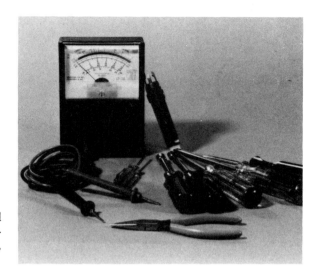

FIG. I—5 Basic tools you'll need: screwdrivers, needle-nose pliers, nut driver set, VOM, IC extractor.

Once you get the screws out, you can troubleshoot and repair your computer with nothing more than a few basic tools. You bought several of them when you bought your computer. The main tool is the computer itself. An ordinary multimeter will help you perform various tests to spot the exact cause of the trouble. With this book as a guide, and using your own intelligence, you have just about everything you need.

Unlike so many machines of "modern" manufacture, almost nothing in the Macintosh requires a special or expensive tool (except for the holding screws, as mentioned above). Chances are you already have all the tools you need. If you don't, the cash outlay to equip yourself will be small.

1. Screwdrivers—Using nothing more than a standard screwdriver, Torx head driver, and small- and medium-headed Phillips (with insulated handles to protect yourself), you can just about completely disassemble your Macintosh. The keyboard is held together with screws; the system board is held with screws; the drives are kept in place and held together by screws. There is very little in the computer that doesn't come apart with a tug of the fingers or a twist of an ordinary screwdriver.

2. Needlenose pliers—You'll rarely need regular pliers. However, having a needlenose at hand makes retrieving dropped parts easier. They also help to remove parts that are being desoldered.

3. Nut drivers—Nut drivers are like fixed socket wrenches. Although none of the screws on the computer have hex heads, the screws on some peripherals can be removed and installed with either the screwdriver or a hex nut driver. Quite often a nut driver makes removal and replacement of the bolts, nuts, and screws easier, faster, and safer. They are also handy when working on certain peripherals, such as printers.

4. Multimeter—To test for voltages, to measure component values, and to check for continuity you will need a good quality multimeter (Fig. i-6). It

FIG. I—6 The multimeter doesn't have to be fancy.

doesn't have to be a fancy digital multimeter. Voltages measured will be in the 5 and 12 volt DC ranges, and 120 AC. It should also be capable of measuring resistance (in ohms). Accuracy *is* important, especially when measuring voltages. If you're not familiar with the use of a multimeter, practice using it before probing inside the computer. For example, take readings of the various outlets in your home to check for AC voltage. Use the meter to check some batteries (DC voltage). If you have some old resistors lying around, check these for correct resistance. It doesn't take long to learn how to use it efficiently and accurately.

5. IC tool—Some of the ICs (integrated circuits) on some boards in your computer or its peripherals are plugged into sockets. Replacement of these is a simple job, but a risky one if you try to do it with your fingers alone. The many prongs (pins) of the IC are easily damaged. An extractor (Fig. i-7) is used to remove the chip from its socket safely.

6. Hex wrench set—Some of the screws, such as those that hold the drives in place, have hexagonal heads. To remove these devices you'll have to have a set of hex wrenches (sometimes called Allen wrenches).

OPTIONAL TOOLS

With the screwdrivers, nut drivers, and the multimeter you'll be able to take care of almost any problem. Other tools, such as those listed below, are merely to make the job easier.

1. Digital soldering tool—If you intend to change single components, you will have to have a high-quality soldering tool, one designed specifically for digital circuits. If you will not be replacing soldered components, you

FIG. I—7 A typical IC tool.

won't need this tool, and you can put off the investment (about $50) until you need it. The tool should have a rating of no higher than 40 watts. If possible, the tip should be grounded to avoid electrical damage to delicate components.

2. Desoldering tool—This is a fancy name for a heat-resistant syringe. Its function is to suck away solder from a heated joint. (You may even hear this tool being called a "solder sucker.") Without it, removing components is possible, but difficult.

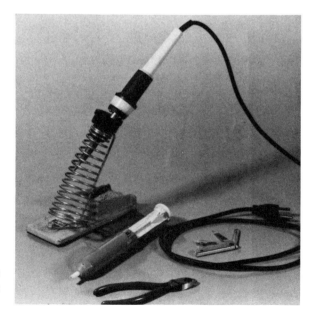

FIG. I—8 Optional tools: soldering and desoldering tools, wire cutters, and knife.

TABLE I–1. Required and Optional Tools

Part	Part Number	Approximate Cost
Screwdriver (blade)	any	$2.50–$6.00
Screwdriver (Phillips)	any	$2.50–$6.00
Screwdriver (Torx)	T-15	$2.00–$12.00
Multimeter (VOM)	RS 22-201	$19.95
IC extractor/installer	RS 276-1574	$6.95
Needlenose pliers	any	$5.00–$10.00
Nut drivers	RS 64-1800	$4.99
Hex wrench set	RS 64-1849	$1.99
Soldering tool (Weller)	TC201 & TC202	$79.95
Desoldering tool	RS 64-2085	$8.79
Wire cutter	RS 64-1841	$3.79
Knife	any	varies
Alignment tools	RS 64-2220	$2.99
Cleaner/degreaser	RS 64-2322	$1.99

3. Wire cutter—New components often have metal leads that are too long. This means that they must be clipped to the proper length. A wire clipper handles this job correctly and efficiently. Some pliers have built-in clippers. These may be suitable for cutting wire but are not meant to trim the leads of components that are soldered in place.

4. Knife—A small, sharp knife can be used for many jobs. Used correctly it can be a valuable tool.

5. Alignment tools—It's rare that the video will need to be realigned, and it's far better to leave this job to a professional. However, if you wish to handle it yourself, a set of plastic alignment tools is essential. The only ones that will work are those that are all plastic. Do not get or use alignment tools that have metal tips. These cause subtle changes in the flow of current in certain adjustable components, which makes alignment impossible.

The items listed in Table I-1 are examples of the tools described in the text. "RS" denotes that the part is available at Radio Shack at a competitive price. Anything equivalent will work as well. Pay attention to the quality of the tools you buy. Some have a thin metal plating that can flake off. These flakes can get down inside the computer and cause a variety of serious problems.

You may also find that an assembled tool kit will suit your needs, such as the one available from Heath Company (# GHP-1270, $39.95). Radio Shack carries a smaller but adequate tool set for $14.95 (# 64-2801). This set lacks a Phillips head screwdriver and hex wrenches, however.

Most of the tools do not have to be specifically for electronics. For example, the screwdriver or pliers you use to work on the car will do just fine (as long as they are clean!).

Chapter 1
Best Results/Minimal Time

Have you ever watched a child take apart a toy? The usual way is for the pieces to go flying in all directions, without any order or planning. Parts that don't come off easily are broken off. Some roll under the couch; others get stepped on; some just disappear.

When it comes to reassembling the toy, the child rarely has the slightest idea of what to do or how to do it. That's when the child brings it to mommy or daddy with big, sad, wet eyes and says, "My toy broke. Fix it for me."

A fair number of computer repair jobs are a direct result of an adult "child" getting inside his electronic "toy" to find out how it works or to attempt a repair. Quite often what started out as a minor problem turns into something expensive.

Sure, you can save hundreds of dollars a year by doing your own repairs and maintenance and by installing any add-on equipment yourself. Approach it incorrectly, however, and it can end up costing many times what the repair should have cost—sometimes in ways you didn't expect.

The Macintosh is designed to keep the end user out of the cabinet. The screws that hold it together have a special Torx head and require a Torx driver. Two of these screws are set back under the handle and cannot be reached with a standard length blade. In addition to this problem, the case is held together tightly and should really only be taken apart with yet another special tool. (See the "Tools" section at the end of the Introduction.)

Care must be exercised at all times. If you rush, you increase the chances of permanently damaging the computer. The problem is greater with the Macintosh than with most other computers, simply because it is designed to discourage the users from going inside.

NEVER attempt to get inside the computer or any peripheral that is still under warranty.

YOUR SAFETY

Nothing is more important than your safety. If you do something that destroys a circuit in the computer, you can replace the circuit. If you let something happen to you—well, there are no such things as replacement parts.

There are actually very few danger spots in your computer. Even while the computer is in operation, the voltage inside (past the power supply and excluding the CRT monitor) is either 5 volts DC or 12 volts DC. The amount of current flowing through most of the circuit is so tiny that you wouldn't even feel it.

The DC power used in the operation of most digital circuits isn't at all dangerous. However, there are certain places where the voltage and current aren't quite so safe. These spots are usually where AC power comes into the device. Touch one of these places and you're in for a bad time.

The power supply is exposed, along with several hot spots on that board. It's all too easy to come into contact with 120 live (and deadly) AC volts, or with the thousands of volts being supplied to the CRT. For example, as you reach to make an adjustment to the video board, the back of your hand may brush against the fuse block or against the CRT flyback coil.

The Macintosh uses an internal CRT monitor. To operate, more than 10,000 volts are needed. Although the current is quite low, the combination of that current and that voltage is potentially deadly. Worse yet, the CRT has the tendency to store up this charge. Even if you shut off the power and unplug the machine, the dangerous charge will still be present.

This charge can be drained off by shorting the high voltage lead to ground, which reduces the danger. However, it is best to leave any fiddling or testing of the CRT to someone who knows how to safely handle the high voltages. In brief—STAY AWAY!

EFFECTS OF CURRENT

The line coming into the power supply of your computer, and into most peripherals, is 120 volts AC. The amperage can be as high as the physical limits of the wire and the circuit breaker or fuse. Usually this means that the line is 120 volts with a current of at least 15 amps steady, plus a surge limit in the hundreds of amps. This is enough power to melt a metal rod, and more than enough power to kill.

Tests were done by the U.S. Navy to learn the effects of alternating current (AC) with a frequency of 60 cycles per second. (The measure of frequency is sometimes made in *hertz*, with one hertz being the same as one cycle per second, or cps.) It was found that a tiny trickle of just 1 milliamp (.001 amps, or one one-thousandth of an amp) would produce a shock that could be felt. A current of 10 milliamps (.01 amps, or one one-hundredth of an amp) would cause the muscles to become paralyzed, making it impossible for the person to let go of the source of the shock. In fact, the spasms caused

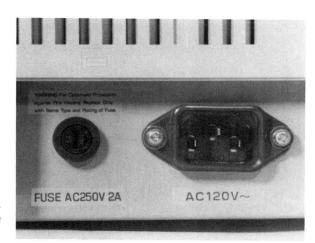

FIG. 1–1 Be very careful around any spot where there is an AC voltage.

by this amount of current can cause the person to grip the source more tightly. At 100 milliamps (one tenth of an amp) the shock is usually fatal if it continues for more than a second.

As you can see, it doesn't take much current to bring on a severe hazard. If you carelessly touch a hot spot you will become a part of the power circuit. For a short time (until the fuse or circuit breaker pops) the current flows unhampered. You risk having a surge of perhaps a hundred amps flow

FIG. 1–2 There are 120 deadly volts passing through that fuse when the power is on.

FIG. 1—3 The flyback coil is another danger spot inside the Macintosh.

FIG. 1—4 The internal CRT is dangerous in several ways. It's best to leave any problems, diagnosis, or work to a professional.

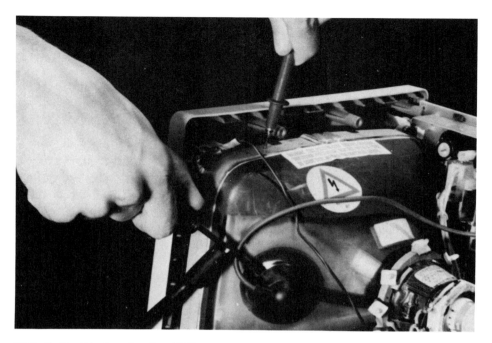

FIG. 1—5 Discharging the CRT.

through your body, which is over 1000 times as much as is needed to be fatal.

DANGER SPOTS

Any spot with AC current presents a risk for you. Most of these spots are obvious and are easy to avoid. The danger begins with the wall outlet (or the circuit box if you ever get to fooling around there). It moves up through the wires and into the power switches.

The wires come into the equipment and are connected in such a way as to make it difficult to touch the contacts. However, you might touch them accidentally if you're not careful. The power supply is one of the two serious electrical dangers to you inside the computer, since the line voltage enters the computer here. (The CRT is the other.) Repair of the power supply is normally handled by replacement. You should not attempt to repair it. There is also another danger within the power supply circuitry, namely the filter capacitors.

Past the switch and within the power supply are small "cans." These are capacitors. One of their functions is to help change the incoming AC to the needed DC. The AC comes into the power supply where it is changed by a transformer in value to the 5 volts and 12 volts needed. The filter capacitor helps to smooth out the flow. To do this it stores up current as it comes in, and then lets it flow out again in a steady stream.

The Most Dangerous Spots

1. *Wall outlet*
2. *Power cord*
3. *Power switches*
4. *Power supply*

5. *CRT (monitor)*
6. *Filter capacitors*
7. *Printer and mechanical parts*

Even after the computer is shut off, and even with the power cord pulled from the outlet, the capacitors can have a hefty charge inside. Theoretically they should drain themselves of all charge in a matter of seconds. Normally there is no danger. But if something should go wrong with the circuitry, you won't know it until you touch the capacitor contacts—at which point you'll find out all too quickly.

The Macintosh and most peripherals have power going directly to the switches. (With the computer, it passes through an AC filter and a fuse, but it is still hot at the switch.) It is a common misconception that a switch is safe when it is in the "off" position. It is not safe unless the power cord has been removed from the outlet. If you happen to touch the incoming contacts, it would be the same as if you grabbed the bare power lines or stuck your fingers in the wall socket.

With the switch "off," there is no current flowing through the circuitry or device beyond (assuming that everything is functioning properly). A fuse cannot do this. It is there for the protection of the circuits inside, not for your protection. If a short circuit happens, the power supply will begin to draw large amounts of current. In a very short time this increased flow can cause serious damage. It could also cause a fire. The fuse helps to prevent this from happening.

If the fuse is rated at 2 amps, this simply means that if the current reaches a level higher than this, the fuse wire will melt and current will not flow beyond the fuse. For a fraction of a second more current *can* flow, however. Worse, if you create a short circuit across the fuse, that fuse will do nothing at all. Your body, the screwdriver, or whatever becomes the new fuse. Normally this means that you're once again grabbing a bare wire with 120 volts and temporarily unlimited current.

With the power switched to "off," you can usually safely change an internal fuse, that fuse holder, and other power handling components inside

There is rarely a need to fool with the power supply. Repair is handled by replacing the entire unit.

Chilton's Guide to Macintosh Repair and Maintenance
BEST RESULTS/MINIMAL TIME

the power supply. (Better yet, shut off the switch and unplug the computer or peripheral.) This again assumes that the switch is operating correctly, that the wires are all connected as they should be connected, and that there are no other dangerous parts or wires near the fuse. To work on an external fuse, the switch, or the incoming filter, unplug the computer from the wall, and then let the unit sit for a minimum of 6 hours.

Before you begin, take a moment to get out the voltmeter to make sure there is no voltage present.

The monitor is another source of high voltage. There is the 120 volts AC coming to it. This is a danger in itself. As already mentioned, the danger doesn't stop here.

The monitor is a CRT (cathode ray tube) which works by throwing electrons at the phosphor coated screen. This requires a considerable charge. Generally, the larger the monitor, the larger will be the voltage required to form an image. Even a small monochrome monitor, such as the one in the Macintosh, will require a few thousand volts. The current (amperage) is low, but this doesn't make the monitor safe.

The built-in monitor of the Macintosh reduces the risk and increases it at the same time. It reduces it because the monitor is small and requires a relatively small voltage to operate. It increases the risk because the CRT and its circuitry are right there where you can bump or touch them while working inside the cabinet. Be extremely careful while working anywhere near the monitor and the related circuits.

The monitor brings yet another danger, and one that has nothing to do with electricity. The screen tube has a vacuum inside and thin glass walls. Striking the tube can cause an implosion. Bumping the neck of the tube is even more dangerous. Either can cause very sharp slivers of glass to be thrown around, each of them coated with the phosphor.

FIG. 1–6 The neck of the CRT is especially sensitive to bangs and knocks. The connector you see in this photo should be left alone. It carries high voltage and will hold the charge even with the power off.

FIG. 1–7 This connector carries high voltage for the CRT deflection coils. Leave it alone!

MEASURING VOLTAGE

Although most equipment manufacturers do their best to reduce the risks of accidents, you still have to be careful. I've never heard of it happening with the Macintosh itself, but there have been cases when electronic equipment, such as peripherals, have been shipped with the power wires connected in the wrong order. A "hot" was connected to a spot which should have been "dead." A technician who assumed that everything was as it should be could be in for a shock, literally.

If you are going to be working on the main lines coming into a piece of equipment, the power switches or anywhere that an AC current might be present, don't take the chance that the spot or contact is dead just because it is supposed to be. Measure the voltage. Better yet, unplug the equipment and then measure.

Don't trust anything unless you've measured it and know that no current is present. Even then, be careful. This rule applies whenever you're working around something electrical.

Testing for "hot" is easy to learn if you don't already know how. With a voltmeter or other testing device, touch one probe (usually black) to a known ground, such as the metal chassis of the power supply. Be sure to hold the

FIG. 1—8 Learn how to use a voltmeter.

probe only by the insulated handle. The other probe (usually red) gets touched to the suspected point. Assuming that the meter is functioning properly and that you've put it into the proper testing range, it will tell you if a charge is present and how large that charge is. You can also test for an existing current by touching the two probes across the device (such as touching the two contacts of a switch).

Setting the meter to the correct range is important. If you intend to measure the voltage at the monitor screen, don't have the meter set for 3 volts. (The setting should be in the thousands of volts.) If you're testing for AC, don't have the meter adjusted to test for DC. You're asking for trouble if you just jam the probes inside the computer without first looking to see if the meter is properly set.

RULES OF SAFETY

Working around electricity demands a set of safety rules. The first step is to shut off the power. The main switch will cut the flow to parts farther in. It doesn't protect you completely, though, since the wires between the switch and the wall outlet are still "hot," and because there are certain stored charges inside the computer.

You might think that the best way to protect yourself completely would be to unplug the computer. This is true, with reservations. While pulling the plug does remove the current coming in from the wall outlet, it also removes the safety of a ground wire. This is more to prevent damage to the computer than to yourself. Whether you unplug the computer or not depends on the circumstances. (Normally it's best to unplug.)

With or without the plug, assume that all circuits are live and carry a potentially dangerous current. (The vast majority do not, but if you treat them as if they do you are unlikely to cause damage to either the computer or to yourself.)

You can't see electricity, nor can you tell by sight if a circuit is hot (active). The only immediate indication of power flowing inside the computer is the soft hum of the cooling fan (if you have one), which is easy to ignore once you become accustomed to it. Normally the screen will show something on it, but just because the screen is blank doesn't necessarily mean that there is no current flowing.

By making voltage measurements you assure that you're not sticking your fingers in places where damage will be done—damage to you or to the computer.

Never probe or poke inside the computer with any part of your body touching a conductive surface. Avoid leaning on the chassis, a metal work bench, or anything made of metal if you are reaching inside. Also take care that your feet aren't touching anything conductive (which includes a damp floor). In short, insulate yourself from your surroundings and from the equipment.

Personal Safety Rules

1. *Probe carefully*
2. *Don't touch conductive surfaces*
3. *Observe the one-hand rule*
4. *Use only insulated tools*
5. *Beware of jewelry, hair, neckties, loose clothing*
6. *Moving parts can be dangerous*

To further protect yourself use the "one hand rule." This means, simply, don't reach in with both hands at the same time. Most often the rule states that one hand should be kept in a pocket. This is to avoid the temptation of breaking the rule. If one hand is in a pocket, you almost have to consciously remove it to reach inside the machine.

The idea behind this rule is to prevent your body from becoming a part of a circuit. If just one hand touches a spot and your body is insulated from all conductive surroundings, the current has nowhere to go. If a second hand touches a hot spot, the current can enter the one hand, pass through your body, and out through the other hand.

Another rule is to turn the back of the hand to any potential hot spot. The reason for this is the physical reaction you have to a shock. The muscles contract. If the fingers contract around the source of the shock it will be much more difficult to break free. However, if the contraction is away from the source, the contraction could actually free you from the shock.

Any and all tools should have insulated handles. Touch the tools only by these handles. It's sometimes tempting to grab a part of the blade of a screwdriver for better control, for example. Don't do it! The insulation is on the handle for a reason.

Many people realize that grabbing a tool by the metal is foolish, and then forget about the necklace, ring, or watchband they are wearing. Metal jewelry will conduct current just as well as the shaft of a screwdriver, even better if it's made of gold or silver. A dangling necklace might also become entangled in some mechanical part.

The only moving part in the computer to worry about is the cooling fan (if there is one), but you're unlikely to catch yourself in it. Peripherals are another matter. Printers in particular are loaded with moving parts. Most have a tag inside warning you to remove jewelry and to be careful of long hair. (Having it yanked out by an angry printer is no way to get a haircut.)

There is no such thing as being *too* safe. Just when you think that you've taken every possible precaution, look for something you may have forgotten.

COMPUTER SAFETY

Once you've taken the necessary precautions to protect yourself, you can begin to think about the well-being of the computer. As with personal safety, computer safety is basically a matter of common sense. Rules of thumb such as, "Don't punt the computer across the room no matter how angry you get," and "Don't resort to your hunting rifle just because you're losing at Pac-Man," are obvious (or should be, although you'd be surprised at some of the things people have done to their computers). Other rules are just as obvious if you take a moment to think them out.

In certain ways the computer is a surprisingly tough piece of machinery. If it operates for the first week or so, it's unlikely that anything major will go wrong for many, many years—unless you cause it. Even if you do make some

Computer Safety Rules

1. *Shut off power.*
2. *Take notes, make sketches.*
3. *Don't be in a hurry.*
4. *Never force anything.*
5. *Use the proper tools.*

6. *Avoid short circuits.*
7. *Check for screws, etc.*
8. *Beware of static.*
9. *Open the case carefully, or not at all.*

mistakes in operating or repairing the computer, chances are good that you won't do too much damage.

This doesn't mean that you can be careless. Just as you assume that all circuits are holding deadly charges just waiting to get at you, assume that any mistake will cause the immediate destruction of a $500 circuit. (It *is* possible.)

Again, there is no such thing as being *too* careful.

PHYSICAL DAMAGE

The most common damage done by the do-it-yourselfer is physical. Physical damage is also the least necessary. There is no reason or excuse for it. By being in a hurry, by losing patience, or from carelessness, the wrong thing is done at the wrong time and something snaps.

Most of the parts of your computer are tough. Others can be damaged all too easily. Caution is the key at all times.

Getting inside the case is a good example of where you can get into trouble easily. First, special screws are used. A Torx head screwdriver (size T-15) is needed to get them out. Some people have damaged the case by tugging away at it, not knowing that all the screws have not been removed. There are three "hidden" screws. One of these is in the battery compartment. Two more are tucked away beneath the handle. As mentioned in the Introduction, these two require a longer shaft on the screwdriver.

Although it's possible to separate the case by hand or with a rigged tool, it's best to use the tool made specifically for that job (see Fig. i-3). If you can't find one, be extremely careful in using anything else.

When removing a cord or connector, do so with slow and steady pressure. These are supposed to be somewhat tight in order to maintain a reliable contact, but they're not in so tight as to require the strength of both arms and a foot. If it doesn't move, there is usually a logical reason.

One computer operator decided that the signal cable connectors to the external disk drive was too difficult to remove. He took the probe of his

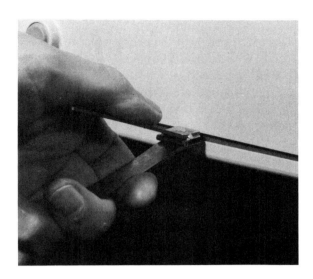

FIG. 1–9 If you must re-move the case, do so care-fully.

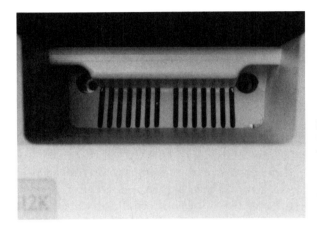

FIG. 1–10 There are three "hidden" screws that hold the case together. One is in-side the battery compart-ment. Two that are difficult to reach are beneath the han-dle, as shown here.

voltmeter and jammed it into the slots of the cable to widen them. Then he was amazed that the operation of the drive was sporadic, at best. He ended up having to replace the cable at a premium cost.

NEVER force anything. Take the few extra seconds to find out why the board, component, or whatever won't move easily.

The components inside your computer have anywhere between 2 and 64 connectors. Each of these leads is prone to physical damage, mostly from bending them too far. The ICs (or *chips*) are particularly sensitive. The ICs have a number of metal prongs coming from them. More often than not the prongs on a new IC are in the wrong positions for easy installation. Bending them manually is the usual solution for the computer owner who is install-ing chips. This brings in the danger of bending the prongs too far (or too little), and then having to bend and rebend the prongs.

Due to the thinness of the prongs, this bending and rebending creates stress on the metal. The prong may break off. It may also crystallize in such a way that the current flow changes, making a seemingly good chip useless.

Most chips you will come across in the Macintosh and related equipment will be soldered into place. Trying to replace one brings the additional danger of destroying the chip, and the board, with heat. There are special tools made to help unsolder chips, but these can get to be expensive since you have to have the proper sizes.

The simplest solution is to leave the job to a professional. There are too many dangers in attempting it yourself unless you are skilled with soldering and desoldering. The few dollars you save in doing the job yourself can literally go up in smoke.

USE THE PROPER TOOLS

The solution to this and to related problems is to use the proper tools for the job at hand. If the chips are socketed, two special tools are available to handle the delicate chips. One is made to put the prongs into the correct places for installation (an "IC installer"). The other is designed to aid in the removal of chips (an "IC extractor"). Both tools are fairly expensive for someone who plans to install or remove just one chip per decade. Both are inexpensive when you consider the cost per ruined chip. If you have some equipment with socketed chips and want to reduce the risk, at least get an IC extractor.

These tools offer an additional safeguard. Some chips are extremely sensitive to static. Your body has the tendency to store up static charges. You have probably experienced a tiny shock when touching a doorknob or other metal object after walking across a rug. If the charge was enough for you to feel, it was more than enough to fry the insides of a delicate chip. Even a static charge you cannot feel can be enough to ruin a chip.

The IC extracting and installing tools will help prevent this from happening. You can reduce static build up by treating the carpets, either with a commercial product or with a dilute mixture of water and standard fabric softener. You can also make use of a "static discharge device." This is a device connected to a ground (such as a neutral screw on a wall outlet). You touch a metallic spot with your finger, and any static charge your body might have is drained off safely.

SHORT CIRCUITS AND OHM'S LAW

The second most common type of damage done during repair is caused by short circuits. This can happen in several different ways.

The usual way is by touching the metal tip of a tool or probe across two points that are not meant to be connected. Most often this won't matter. Other times it will send a circuit off into oblivion with a cloud of smoke.

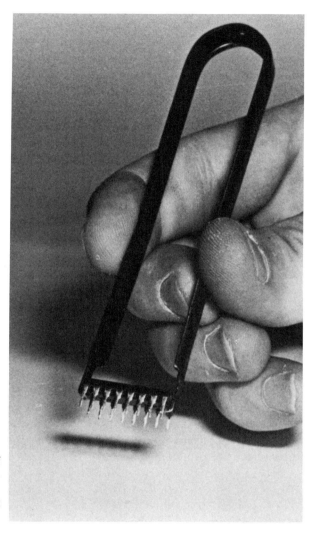

FIG. 1–11 The prongs of an IC are delicate and the inside can be ruined by static. *Handle with care:* use an IC extractor for removal.

There is a mathematical relationship between voltage, amperage, and resistance. This is stated by *Ohm's Law*. The formula for this law is "E = I × R." E is the voltage, I is current in amps, and R is resistance in ohms. If you multiply the current times the resistance, you'll know the voltage.

With some basic algebra you find that R = E/I and I = E/R. By sticking some numbers into that last formula, you can see what happens with a short circuit. It simply states that the current flowing is equal to the voltage divided by the resistance.

The voltage remains constant due to the design of the power supply. In most circuits this will be 5 volts. If the resistance is 10,000 ohms, the current flowing is .0005 amps. A short circuit effectively drops this resistance to near zero, which means that the current will flow to the limit allowed by the power supply (often 2 amps or more). For computer circuits designed to handle just fractions of a milliamp, the effect can be disastrous—like trying to instantly force a few hundred gallons of water through a tiny hose meant to carry just a few ounces.

In the previous section there was mention of necklaces and other jewelry causing current to flow into your body. While working inside the computer itself there isn't enough current flow to cause any harm to you. However, the rule about jewelry applies—this time to protect the computer.

If that necklace swings down and creates an electronic bridge, you may not be able to feel the effect, but the computer probably will. Resistance drops to near zero. As a result, current swings in the other direction.

The human body normally has a very high resistance. Unless your hands are wet, touching an active circuit inside is unlikely to cause any damage. (This means a digital circuit, not one of those that carry high voltage or AC.) A ring on your finger or a watch on your wrist is another matter. The metal will act the same as if you had connected a wire from spot to spot. All these are fairly easy to keep track of. Pay attention to what you're doing and you should have no problems.

Other things that are more difficult to notice can also cause shorts. When taking things apart, keep careful track of the various screws, bolts, nuts, and other metal parts. Take notes and make drawings if you think they are needed. It's all too easy for a part to fall inside the computer unnoticed, only to cause trouble later on. When you turn on the power, that forgotten chunk of threaded metal becomes a surprisingly efficient conductor.

Less likely, but still possible, are small shreds of metal falling inside the computer. The average computer owner won't have to worry about these unless a screw has been forced (which could strip off a piece of the thread) or unless the lead of a component has broken off.

PREVENTING ELECTRICAL DAMAGE

To prevent accidental short circuits, flip the switch to cut off the power before removing anything. There is only one reason for the power to be on while working inside the computer, and that is for testing, probing, and measuring (and those must be done carefully). For anything else, the power should be off and should remain off. Make shutting down the power your automatic response, and applying power what you stop and think about.

Imagine yourself going inside the computer for a simple repair, such as to replace a socketed chip. You forget the rule and leave the power on. You're being careful and use an IC extractor, but touch the metal tool to active circuits ("zzzt, zzzt, zzzt"). The faulty chip is pulled and you go to install the new one. You've been careful about reinstallation and know that everything is where it is supposed to be. But nothing works. You scratch your head and say, "Now how could that have happened?"

This isn't likely to happen. What is important is that it *could* happen. If a board or component is removed while current is flowing through it, the current value often changes. As the value changes in one place, other changes will take place elsewhere. Small changes probably won't cause damage, although they can cause the circuit to "age." Larger sudden changes have effects similar to those of short circuits or static discharge, namely they destroy the circuit from the inside.

When working inside the computer (with the power off!) pay attention to what you are doing. Look carefully at any connector you are going to remove. Make notes and sketches so you have something for reference. (Keep these notes and sketches handy for future times when you want to get inside the computer.) Before you turn the power on again, look around inside. Are all the connectors back in their proper places? Have you left any screws, nuts or bits of metal inside?

COMPONENT REPLACEMENT

Most of the time a component failure will be handled by replacing an entire board. Even professional technicians use this method of repair. It may sound as though this might be more expensive. Actually it is not. Tracking down a problem to a single component is time consuming, and often the time involved ends up costing more than a new board.

Added to this is the difficulty in replacing some of the components. Chips soldered into place present special problems. Even if you have the skill and tools for safe replacement, you may not be able to find the proper replacement parts.

Since you probably do not have the equipment or skill that the technician has, you will probably confine most repairs to board replacement rather than component replacement. (When you handle the repair by replacement, keep in mind that the malfunctioning board or unit has a trade-in value.)

There will be times when you will be able to identify the exact component and will want to replace just this piece. When this is possible, the savings to you are large. Most of the components in your computer cost very little. Diodes, resistors, and capacitors cost just pennies. The ICs are often just a few dollars. Many of the ICs used in the computer can be purchased for under a dollar. (Others can't be purchased for any price.)

The first rule when dealing with component replacement is to make certain that the new component is exactly the same as the one it replaces. If you're uncertain about which parts are which or how to read the component values, pick up a book on basic electronics.

Some components have polarity. An electrolytic capacitor, such as the filter capacitor in the power supply, has positive and negative leads. Install a new one backwards and it could explode. Other components won't react so violently but could cause damage throughout the circuit. Expensive damage. ICs that are not installed correctly can burn up and may take a whole string of other components and circuits with them.

Even when you aren't replacing a component, pay attention to polarity.

Many repairs require disconnecting cables and other wires. Most of these have special keyed plugs, making it impossible to reconnect them with the wrong polarity. But you may run into a few that don't have this intelligent design.

Taking notes and making sketches are important parts of any repair. Get into the habit, even when you don't think that you'll need the notes and drawings. There is no need to be a professional artist or writer. What you do is primarily for your own use and a jog to your memory. Assume, though, that others might need to use them. It's possible that you'll have to consult a pro on the repair. The notes and drawings could save you quite a bit of time and money.

SOLDERING

Some components plug into place. Depending on which mainboard is installed in your Macintosh and which peripherals you own, you may have quite a few socketed ICs. On other boards many are soldered into place. On both, the other components are soldered.

Despite what you might think, soldering is an art. It's not a skill you can learn in a few minutes. With circuits as critical as those of a computer, you certainly shouldn't be practicing inside your computer. There are a number of books and pamphlets available on how to solder. Heath Company offers a course in soldering. Before you even consider soldering inside the computer, learn everything you can about it. Then practice, practice, practice.

The soldering iron used for digital circuits, such as those in the Mac, should be rated at no more than 30 to 40 watts. In fact, 40 watts is almost too much. Anything hotter could too easily damage the circuit or the board. Even with the lower powered iron, anything more than a few seconds of contact is risky. Many components are very heat sensitive. The internal goodies can all too easily be fried. The board may also be damaged permanently. If this happens, you may as well scrap the board and buy a new one.

The soldering iron should be designed specially for digital soldering. These irons are more expensive, but the extra cost is a necessity. They have grounded tips, which prevents damage from any build up of electrical charge. Don't try to use any old soldering iron or gun for the job.

To remove a component, especially one with many contacts (such as an IC), be sure to use a desoldering tool. This inexpensive device removes the melted solder from the contacts, making it possible to simply pull the old component loose. Move slowly and carefully so as not to cause damage. The more contacts the component has, the trickier it is to remove it.

In many cases, it is easier and sometimes less expensive to destroy the chip installed by clipping each of the leads, and then removing the tiny pins one at a time. Heating each of the leads on a whole chip to remove the solder increases the possibility of damaging the board. Often, to get the chip out,

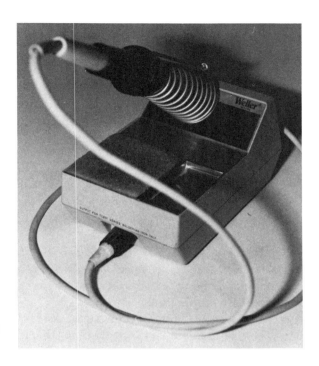

FIG. 1–12 A soldering tool for digital circuits.

you'll have to heat and reheat each prong. You're almost certain to ruin the chip itself with excess heat, especially if you're not a master at soldering.

Before you destroy a chip—before you bring a soldering iron anywhere near the computer—be sure that it is a last resort. You'll be better off at this point to turn the job over to someone who knows how to handle the task, and who will guarantee the work. This guarantee should be for a minimum of 90 days.

PREPARING TO WORK

Before you begin any repair you should have a solid understanding of the correct procedure. Diagnosis and repair is a logical sequence of steps. (More on this in Chapter 2.) Learn these steps. Follow them! They'll save you money, time, frustration, and a whole lot of trouble.

The first step is so simple that most people ignore it. Make backups of every bit of software. Many books and courses suggest this and mention making a copy. Instead, make at least *two* copies. Having the original plus the two copies helps to protect you in a number of ways.

Software losses can occur due to fire, water, forgetfulness, and so forth. These should always be of concern to you, however unlikely they might seem at the moment. Losses through the machine are more common.

In one large computer repair house a technician fed in a working disk. There was a problem with the disk drive. The result was that the machine

Protect Yourself

1. *Make at least two backup disks.*
2. *Test the backups.*
3. *Store the original and one backup safely.*

"ate" the diskette. His solution was to feed in a second diskette. The computer destroyed this one as well. So he booted up a third; then a fourth. By the time he figured out that the drive was annihilating the recorded programs, five copies were destroyed.

This may sound silly. A professional *should* know better. The average operator may not. If the problem is intermittent, it would be very easy for even the most experienced operator to waste a program or two before realizing what the problem is.

After making your two backups, perform an accuracy test. Run each copy to be sure that it works properly or that it contains the correct data. The testing at the time of making the copy is a step that should always be taken. Without it you don't know for certain if your copy is a copy or is just a useless diskette.

If the day comes that your machine doesn't accept the original diskette, check it with a copy. If this copy doesn't work, chances are good that something is wrong with the drive. If the malfunction has erased the first two, you have the third to protect yourself.

WHERE IS THE PROBLEM?

Computers are extraordinarily reliable. Most people have come to think of machines as being at fault when something goes wrong. In many cases this is true. If a car suddenly stalls on the freeway, it is usually a machine error. If a television or radio refuses to work, it is usually the fault of the equipment. With a computer the fault is more often with the person running it.

Most common household equipment is designed so that anyone can operate them. There aren't many things for the operator to change or vary. A television, for example, has very few controls. The owner can switch it on, change the channel, and change the contrast and color within limitations. Beyond this, about all the television operator does is to sit back and view the screen.

Operating a computer normally involves pushing a variety of buttons, each of which does a different task. It's like having thousands of controls available instead of just a half dozen. Just as the computer offers more controls it brings many more opportunities for making mistakes.

Chilton's Guide to Macintosh Repair and Maintenance
BEST RESULTS/MINIMAL TIME

Important Questions to Ask Yourself

1. *Has it ever worked?*
2. *Has that function of the program ever worked?*
3. *Do other programs work?*
4. *What is working, and what is not?*
5. *What did I do wrong?*

Before you tear into your computer, make sure that the fault lies with the computer. Chances are good that the fault is your own or is the fault of the programmer. Most malfunctions are not the fault of the computer.

One of the first questions you should ask yourself is, "Has it ever worked?" An untried program may have flaws. Even a known program may have bugs in it. A tried and true program may give out after a number of uses. (Diskettes are well manufactured, but aren't without error, nor do they last forever.) Then there are those programs that you use every day for their normal functions, but which have other capabilities you haven't yet used. When you get around to trying out the other capabilities, you're back to a "Has it ever worked?" question.

Your first suspicion should be with yourself (or the operator of the computer). Software documentation is notorious for being poorly written. Do you (or does the operator) understand how to work the program? Have you read through the instruction manual completely? Are you trying a new function of an old program?

Second in the line of things to suspect is the software itself. If you have backup copies, try one of these. (If you have been using the program successfully and have tested the copies for all functions, you can eliminate the "Has it ever worked?" question.)

Another test is to boot up a different program. For example, if your word processing program isn't working, try your accounting program or one of the games you have. (Be sure to read the manual for that piece of software if you're not already familiar with its operation.)

If you have checked out any possible operator and software failure, the next step is the visual check. Look for what doesn't look right. Don't start pulling boards and components until you've completed this step. Look for the obvious. Much of the time you can solve the problem with very little effort.

Perhaps you've dropped a screw or nut and this is shorting one of the internal circuits. Maybe the clamping mechanism of the disk drive is malfunctioning and won't allow the spindle to make proper contact with the diskette.

Where Is the Fault?

1. *Operator*
2. *Software*
3. *Peripherals*
4. *Disk drives*
5. *Computer*

Notes should be taken throughout. Even before you begin your diagnostics you should have something written down. What is working. What is not? Jot down all the symptoms along with any errors that the computer shows. As you go on with your diagnosis, continue to take notes.

Don't waste your time on parts that are functioning properly. Diagnosis is a process of elimination. If you know for a fact that the drives are accepting the programs, that your printer is operating, and that the monitor is giving a correct image for what is being sent to it, then eliminate or ignore these sections of the computer. If the problem is that the RAM won't hold data, why waste time taking apart the drive? All you can do is to cause more problems.

Begin with the most obvious and the easy. Work you way to the more complex.

All checks begin with the cabinet closed. Make a note of what is happening, or what is not happening. Check and recheck for operator error, then for software error or for diskette failure. Only then should you think about opening the cabinet. You should have at least a fair idea of what you're looking for before opening the cabinet.

When this step comes along, move slowly and deliberately. With the box open look around for the obvious. Don't just start tearing into the computer. All you can cause is damage if you're in too much of a hurry.

AN OUNCE OF PREVENTION . . .

Chapter 7 deals with maintenance. Your Macintosh has been designed and built to require very little maintenance. You can pretty much ignore your machine—almost to the point of abuse—and it will keep going.

There are still some preventive maintenance requirements.

The greatest enemy of the computer is dust. A tiny fleck of dust that your eye can't even see can gouge a diskette and make it useless. Dust combined with humidity can cause short circuits.

Yet dust is everywhere. All you can really do is to reduce the amount that gets into your computer, particularly into the mechanical parts. Some dust on the boards is unlikely to cause any problems. But just a few invisible particles on the disk drive heads can slice the data on a diskette to shreds.

Enemies

1. *Dust*	5. *Other contaminants*
2. *Liquid*	6. *Humidity*
3. *Food*	7. *Weight or pressure*
4. *Smoke*	8. *Carelessness (i.e., you)*

Keep the area around the computer as clean as possible. Do not use a feather duster or anything like it. A slightly damp rag will pick up the dust rather than toss it into the air, where it will do even more damage. Store all diskettes safely, preferably inside a diskette storage box.

One threat you can eliminate entirely is that of food and drink. Make it a policy never to allow anything spillable within a 20-foot radius of the computer. If you or some other operator wants a cup of coffee, it's time for a break *away* from the computer.

Liquids in particular are dangerous. Spilling something into the keyboard may necessitate total replacement of the keyboard, plus repairs inside the computer caused by the short circuits.

SUMMARY

The rules of handling a computer safely are little more than common sense put into practice. If something seems silly, don't do it. If it seems logical and sensible, think it over before you do it.

Don't attempt to do anything unless you have some idea as to what you are doing and how to do it. Likewise, don't attempt a repair without the proper equipment. To put it even more simply, "When in doubt, *don't.*"

The First Steps

1. *Read the book thoroughly*
2. *Read Chapter 1 again (for safety tips)*
3. *Perform diagnosis (Chapter 2)*
4. *Read applicable repair chapter (Chapters 3–6)*
5. *Repair or replace*
6. *Consult a professional if needed (Chapter 9)*
7. *Back in operation again!*

Some problems can be solved immediately, in less time than it takes to call in and wait for a technician. Others may take more time. You'll learn which problems to tackle yourself and which to save for a professional.

In diagnosing problems, suspect yourself first. Next, suspect the software and diskettes. After this begin all checks with the cabinet still closed. Take notes constantly. Make sketches where applicable. Don't trust your memory.

In making repairs, keep in mind that the design of the machine demands exact components. If a resistor goes out, the replacement for that resistor must have exactly the same value.

Finally, read through the entire applicable chapter before you attempt to work on a section of your computer. If you suspect the drives, for example, read Chapters 3 and 4 thoroughly before you begin. (Read Chapter 2 before you do anything!)

Repair and maintenance of a computer is not difficult. People less intelligent than you are doing it every day and without making errors. At the same time, people with more intelligence are messing things up faster than they can be repaired, almost always because they refuse to follow "The Rules."

Chapter 2
Diagnosis: What's Wrong With It?

When something goes wrong with your computer it's tempting to immediately remove the cover and start poking around. Even if you have some idea as to what might be wrong, this is probably the worst way to begin. The cure of a problem *always* begins with the cabinet closed, and usually with the power off.

Diagnosis is a step-by-step process. Often you can skip certain steps. When you do, you should know why you're skipping them. (This will be because the step has taken care of itself automatically, such as checking to see if the computer is plugged in. Obviously you don't have to check this if power is getting to the computer.)

The primary diagnostic steps are covered in this chapter. Once you have tracked a problem to a particular system or device by using these steps, you will be guided to the correct section of the book for further diagnosis and for the final repair or replacement.

For example, imagine that your computer refuses to accept a program. The cause could be many things. This chapter will take you through a diagnosis until you have tracked the problem to a single part of the computer system. If the problem is in the software, you will be instructed at that point to turn to Chapter 3 for more details. if the preliminary diagnosis indicates that the problem is caused by the disk drives, you'll be directed to Chapter 4.

It's as simple as that. When a problem comes up, begin right here in this chapter (unless you already know for sure what is causing the problem). Diagnosis is little more than a process of isolating the cause of the problem. By using this chapter you can eliminate many of the things that are *not* causing the problem. You can then more easily pin down what *is* malfunctioning.

BEFORE OPENING THE CABINET

Most problems and malfunctions can be taken care of without ever taking the computer apart. Many can be spotted and cured without even turning on the power.

There are six steps before you open the cabinet: (1) check for operator error; (2) check for software error; (3) look for the obvious; (4) observe symptoms; (5) take notes; and (6) use the diagnostics diskette, if you have one.

CHECK FOR OPERATOR ERROR

Unlike a television set, a computer has remarkably few hardware malfunctions. If something goes wrong with a television set, the chances are good that the fault lies in the set. After all, there is little chance of operator error. There aren't many knobs to turn or adjust (misadjust might describe it better for malfunctions). The only "programming" is that provided by the local broadcasting companies. Even the new programmable televisions require little on the part of the operator compared to handling a computer.

The computer works because of what the operator does. It has hundreds of controls, generally accessed through the keyboard. The more controls you are required to operate, the more likely you are to mess up somewhere along the way. Then add to this the accidental flubs, such as pressing the wrong key, and you begin to appreciate the differences between handling a computer and the operation of a television set.

If you are the operator, much of the time you'll know when you make a mistake. If the operator is someone other than yourself this may not be true. It's possible that as an operator tries to recover from the error the problem could get worse, making your job of tracking it down more difficult.

Programs you write yourself are excellent examples of how important operator error can be. Each command has to be just right. A program gives directions to the computer and guides it through the complex electronic maze inside. Give it incorrect directions and the computer will get "lost" (shown by the computer giving an error).

Don't think that operator error can only occur with "homebrew" programs. Even software that has been professionally written isn't free of suspicion. (See the next section.) A flawless program can present some very strange troubles if you don't understand its functions, characteristics, and quirks.

Does the operator know how to operate the program? Is it a new program, or perhaps a new feature of a familiar program? (Ask yourself, "Has the program or function *ever* worked?") If you're working with a new program or function, then it's possible that the "malfunction" is nothing more than a lack of knowledge on the part of the operator.

If you could spend some time in a computer repair shop and listen to some of the malfunctions (and their solutions), you'd come to realize just

36

Chilton's Guide to Macintosh Repair and Maintenance
DIAGNOSIS: WHAT'S WRONG WITH IT?

how many things the operator can do wrong. It has nothing to do with being stupid or even careless. Most of the time the problem is due to an honest mistake. One operator was never shown how to start the machine let alone how to run it after it was going. Another had the power cord kicked out by the family dog and couldn't figure out why the computer seemed dead. Still another erased a large amount of valuable data because he thought that the diskettes had to go through the formatting routine each time before trying to load them.

If it's even remotely possible that the problem is operator error, check it out completely before blaming the computer. Of all computer "malfunctions," about a third are brought about by nothing more than operator error. (See Chapter 9.)

CHECK FOR SOFTWARE ERROR

Once you've eliminated the operator as the source of the error, be sure that the software isn't the cause. This includes both the data on the diskettes and the diskettes themselves. Both can produce errors that may seem to be machine problems. Of all problems that come in to a repair shop the vast majority are caused either by operator error or by software error. In a sense, the software becomes a sort of operator once it is fed into the computer. It tells the computer what to do and how to do it when the human operator pushes the various keys.

New programs and diskettes are especially suspect. Just because the box and plastic wrapper are intact doesn't mean that nothing could have happened to it. In some ways the diskettes are as delicate as Christmas tree bulbs (see Chapter 3). Despite all the care and testing, a flaw could have snuck in during the manufacture, or the diskette could have been damaged in transit. A program on the diskette might have been imperfect to begin with, or may have faulty sections. (I have a chess game in which the king cheats whenever he is in trouble.)

Newer programs are more open to suspicion than programs that have been around for a long time. After several thousand users run the program through its paces and find the errors, the manufacturer can release an improved version. (The fact that new programs often contain weaknesses of various sorts isn't necessarily the fault of the manufacturer, although it usually is. Too many software companies use the customers as "beta testers" to find the bugs they should have found before releasing the program.)

Making backup copies of all software and data diskettes is a good way to protect yourself from software failure. You should have at least one backup copy of anything that is important to you. Two copies are better yet. Be sure to test the copy before storing it. Then, if something goes wrong with the original, you'll have a quick means of recovery. You'll also have a way to test to see if the problem is in the software or in the hardware.

LOOK FOR THE OBVIOUS

A new computer owner took his system home, pushed in the program diskette (just as he'd been shown at the shop), but nothing happened. That same afternoon he tucked all the equipment in his car and brought it back in. It operated flawlessly, so he took it back home again, only to have the system refuse to operate again. Next day he was back in the shop.

"I just don't understand it," he said. "I know the outlet is good because I plugged a lamp into it. Maybe something got jiggled inside the computer when it was in the car." Again the system operated perfectly while in the shop, and with the owner standing there watching. Then he saw the technician reach back to flip off the power. "What's that switch for?" he asked.

That may sound silly, but it is a true story. Somehow he managed to get the idea that shoving in the disk automatically kicked in the power. It's such an obvious thing that the sales rep hadn't even bothered to show the customer how to apply power to the computer.

This same customer might have been tempted to rip off the cabinet to see what was the matter. It probably would have done no harm. On the other hand, he could have caused actual damage before he realized that all he had to do was flip a switch.

Look for the obvious before you do anything else. If the computer seems

FIG. 2–1 If the computer is dead, but everything seems normal, don't forget to check the fuse.

Chilton's Guide to Macintosh Repair and Maintenance
DIAGNOSIS: WHAT'S WRONG WITH IT?

38

dead, look to see if the plug is still in the outlet and check to make sure that the power switch has been flipped before tearing apart the power supply.

The same applies to all cables and connectors. It's easy for them to become loose even if your computer sits perfectly still, and especially if you're one of those who prefers merely pushing the connectors into place instead of screwing them in tight. You can't always tell if the connector is secure just by looking, either. Push them in to make sure that contact is being made, and check to see if the screw-in knobs are tight.

The brightness control on the monitor might have been bumped or accidentally turned so that something seems to be wrong. The more people there are who touch your system, the greater the chance that something has been bumped, nudged, or otherwise messed up by human action.

A program refusing to load could be something as simple as having an erased "System" on the diskette, or accidentally having put in the wrong diskette. A flickering on the screen or recording error could be caused by someone in the next room turning on a vacuum cleaner or an electric mixer.

Then there are problems with the physical construction due to normal wear and tear. What might appear to be a major problem with a disk drive could be nothing more than a malfunctioning or sticking disk drive clamping mechanism.

Even inside the cabinet keep your eyes open for the obvious. There are more connectors inside the cabinet. Check each of these carefully (with the power off!). Some peripherals use plug-in expansion boards. The boards may have not been pushed all the way into the expansion slots. A screw may have fallen to cause a short. Even faulty components are sometimes obviously damaged. A capacitor might be leaking fluid, or a resistor might be obviously burned. A soldered connection might be loose or "cold." (If it was you who did the soldering, this possibility is even greater.)

As you're going through the more detailed steps of diagnosis, keep looking for the obvious. Always start with the simple and obvious things, and then go to the more complex.

CHECKING FOR POWER

If all connections seem sound and still nothing happens, it's time to do the first obvious step. Check the incoming power. Checking for power in an outlet is easy. The easiest method is to plug something else into the socket, such as a lamp. If the lamp lights, you know that there is power coming in through the outlet. It won't tell you much more than this, though.

Using a meter is a more accurate gauge. (Set the meter to read in the 120 volt AC range.) It will tell you more than just if power is coming in. Power companies are famous for producing "dirty" power. It has periodic drops and surges. The problem is compounded during peak power times. In the middle of a hot summer afternoon, for example, the power company may be

Chilton's Guide to Macintosh Repair and Maintenance
DIAGNOSIS: WHAT'S WRONG WITH IT?

39

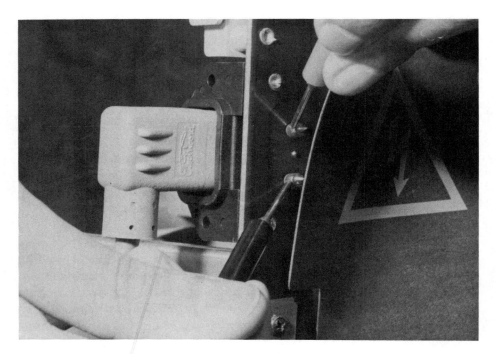

FIG. 2—2 Using a meter to check for incoming power.

having a hard time keeping up with the demand placed on the lines by the thousands of air conditioners going. Line voltage is bound to drop.

The power supply in the Macintosh will easily tolerate any voltage between about 105 and 135 volts. If the voltage goes beyond these limits, a built-in safety circuit will shut everything down. Even at the computer's 105 volt minimum, a lamp will probably work just fine. The lamp *seems* to indicate that the outlet is good, yet the computer will still refuse to function. Using a meter to check the outlet voltage is more certain.

If you have a fan installed, this is an automatic clue. It is usually wired directly to the incoming 120-volt line. If the fan is running, the outlet and power cable are good. The problem is probably in the power supply.

OBSERVE SYMPTOMS

If there is a problem, it will usually show up as soon as you apply power. Observe how the computer comes on while everything is functioning properly.

The normal sequence is for the screen to light up after a short beep and for the "?" icon to appear. Insert the disk you wish to load. The disk drive should give off a sound as it loads in the program or other data. If everything is functioning correctly, the Finder or the screen for your program will appear.

When nothing at all happens, you would usually suspect the power supply. You can find out quickly whether the power supply is at fault. Your first step is to check the obvious. Is power getting to the computer? If the device has an external fuse, check this. If the device (printers often do) has a self test, run this.

Shut off the power, disconnect all external devices possible, and try again. This "unloads" the computer, and reduces the number of things that can drag down the power supply.

If power returns, the problem is either in one of the devices or is a weak power supply. This can be determined by reinstalling each of the devices, one at a time (with the power OFF each time). When power fails again, you'll know which device to suspect. Disconnect everything else and install the suspected device first, then apply power again. If power flows, the power supply is most likely at fault. If it doesn't, the device is the cause.

At this point, you've eliminated everything outside the computer as the possible cause. Again shut off the power. This time open the cabinet, and start looking for the obvious again. If everything is still dead, the problem is either in the power supply (go to Chapter 6) or in the main digital board (go to Chapter 5).

NOTES AND SKETCHES

Throughout the diagnosis process take lots of notes. What is happening? What is not happening? What symptoms are you noticing? If you have to take the computer to a technician later on, those notes will save you time and money. Even if you fix it yourself, the notes will help to guide you along and will also serve for future reference.

The notes should include sketches. This way you'll have an easier time reassembling things after you're finished. Don't trust your memory. It's too easy to forget that screw #17 fits into such-and-such slot to hold this particular thing to that particular thing.

The plugs and connectors are keyed. (This may not be true for certain devices from other manufacturers.) Even so, keep track of which connector goes where. The more you disassemble the more important will be the notes and sketches.

DIAGNOSTICS DISKETTE

Although you can diagnose many malfunctions with just your eyes, common sense, and liberal use of the built-in self test (see the next section), a diagnostic diskette makes the job much easier. The purpose of such a diskette is to help you to spot most problems and to run periodic checks. By using this diskette, and the information contained in this chapter, you'll be able to track down most of the common failures within your system, often down to the individual components.

TABLE 2–1. Troubleshooting Guide

Symptom	Possible Problem	Cure	Chapter
Bell does not beep	Bad speaker or connector	Replace speaker or connector	
	Bad analog board		
	Bad main board	Replace main board	5
No display	Monitor not turned on (if external)	Turn monitor on	8
	No signal to monitor	Check cables	6
	No power to monitor	Check power	6
	Bad monitor	Check monitor	6
	Bad main board	Replace main board	5
Drive LEDs do not come on	Bad or loose connector	Check or replace	4
	No power	Check power	4,6
	Disk drive bad	Check disk drive	4
	Drive controller chip bad	Replace chip	4
	Main board bad	Replace main board	5
Keyboard does not work	Keyboard not plugged in	Plug in keyboard	
	Keyboard faulty	Check keyboard	6
	Keyboard cable or connector bad	Test cable	6
	Main board bad	Replace main board	5
Cannot load in programs		Check the obvious	
	Bad diskette	Try backup	
	No System		
	Drive not working	Check with diags Check drive Replace drive	4
	Bad drive cable or connector	Check drive cable and connectors	4
	Bad memory	Check memory (diags); replace if necessary	5,6
	Bad main board	Replace main board	5

Symptom	Possible Problem	Cure	Chapter
Blinking "X" on screen	No System on diskette		3,4
Mouse does not work	Dirty roller or contacts	Clean mouse	6
	Poor rolling surface		
	Mouse bad	Replace mouse	6
Printer failure	Bad cable or connectors	Check cable and connectors	6
	No power to printer	Check power	2,6
	Cover not in place	Check cover position and on-line light	
	DIP switches not set	Set switches	
	Incompatible printer	Use another printer	
No time, date, or inconsistent	Dead clock battery	Replace battery	

Knowing how to use this diskette correctly can save you many frustrating hours. Why waste hours trying to determine the problem when you have the tool to do so right there in front of you—your own computer? Most machines lack the ability to tell you what's wrong. Your computer *has* this ability, if you know how to use it.

The diagnostics routines on the diskette aren't just for finding problems after they've happened. The diskette should be used on a regular basis, to keep track of how things are inside the computer. It should also be used whenever you've made any change in the system, anytime you've moved the system, or whenever the system has been idle for an extended period of time.

Unfortunately, there are not many diagnostics programs presently available for the end user of the Macintosh. In time, more will almost certainly be available.

The technical advisor for this book, Greg Guerin, has created a special diagnostics program for those readers who are interested. This program contains tests for all the essential systems and functions of the Macintosh. You can order a copy of this valuable program from Tetra, P.O. Box 26275, Tempe, AZ 85282.

The cost for the diagnostics program is $30 for all readers in North America; $35 for those outside North America. This includes all shipping and handling charges. (Arizona residents should also include 6% sales tax,

Chilton's Guide to Macintosh Repair and Maintenance
DIAGNOSIS: WHAT'S WRONG WITH IT?

43

which is $1.80.) To get this special price, you *must* mention this book with your order. Included in the package are the program itself, instruction booklet, and information on how to build the two test loop-backs for checking the external ports. (These loop-back plugs are available for a nominal charge for those not inclined to build their own.)

The program tests (1) RAM, (2) ROM, (3) disk read/write and write protect, (4) keyboard, (5) mouse movement and button, (6) speaker, (7) clock chip and battery, (8) printers, (9) printer port, (10) modem port, (11) screen focus, and (12) screen linearity.

All tests can be accessed individually, or they can be stacked to run any series of tests you wish. Even more important, you can cause any test to cycle as many times as you wish. This is a particularly important feature for testing the chips. Quite often a failing chip won't show up as bad until it has undergone 30 or more testings.

The ROMs in the Macintosh are specialized custom chips. If one fails, you won't be able to walk into the local electronics supply store for a replacement. With a diagnostics program, you should be able to check out the ROMs, and although you may not be able to change the ROM yourself, at least you'll know what the problem is when you bring the computer into the shop for repairs.

The RAM chips are soldered into place inside the Mac, which makes changing them a problem. They are also prone to failure. A diagnostics program should be able to check each of the RAM chips, find out if one or more is bad, and tell you exactly which one(s).

Any diagnostics program should offer you at least this much power. Since I helped (in a small way) to design the diagnostics program offered above, I know that it can do what the average user needs it to do.

BUILT-IN SELF TEST

Each time you turn on or reset your computer, a quick self-test is run on the system. This testing checks the RAM, ROM, and some of the other essential internal chips. It does *not* check the drives, monitor, mouse, or any externally connected devices.

This self-testing takes place automatically. If something fails, the screen will remain blank except for the sad face icon, and usually an error code to indicate what has gone wrong.

To use the self-test to full advantage, you'll have to install the interrupt and reset buttons. There are two ways to activate the built-in diagnostics. One works while the computer has power. This is to press down and hold the interrupt button and then press the reset. You can also hold down the interrupt and apply power, which does the same thing.

Either way, if everything is normal, you'll see the hex code of 0F 000D. If something is malfunctioning, you'll see one of several error codes on the screen. In Table 2–2 you'll find a listing of the first two digits of the error

TABLE 2–2.
Sad Face Icon Error Codes

Code	Meaning
01	Malfunctioning ROM
02	Malfunctioning RAM—bus test
03	Malfunctioning RAM—write test
04	Malfunctioning RAM—Mod3 test
05	Malfunctioning RAM—location
0F	Exception testing—see Table 2–4

TABLE 2–3. RAM Location Chart

Subcode	Chip Location	Bit	Subcode	Chip Location	Bit
001	F5	0	0100	G5	8
002	F6	1	0200	G6	9
004	F7	2	0400	G7	10
008	F8	3	0800	G8	11
0010	F9	4	1000	G9	12
0020	F10	5	2000	G10	13
0040	F11	6	4000	G11	14
0080	F12	7	8000	G12	15

TABLE 2–4. OF Exceptions Subcodes

Code	Meaning	Code	Meaning
0001	Bus error	0008	Trace
0002	Address error	0009	Line 1010 error
0003	Illegal instruction	000A	Line 1111 error
0004	Zero divide error	000B	Other
0005	Check instruction	000C	Nothing
0006	Traps instruction	000D	Normal
0007	Privilege violation		

code and their meanings. This code will be followed by a space and then four more digits and/or characters. These are explained in Tables 2–3 and 2–4.

For example, if the error code reads 05 0001, a RAM problem has been found with the data bit 0 chip located on the main digital board at the coordinates of F5. A code of 0F 0001 means that there is a general bus error.

SUMMARY

Diagnosis is a matter of listing the possible causes, and then eliminating those things that are not at fault until you find the one or two things that *are* causing problems. This is not nearly as difficult as it sounds. You have all the "tools" you'll need already.

Most problems have nothing to do with the computer or its devices. By careful observation you should be able to find out if the malfunction is

Chilton's Guide to Macintosh Repair and Maintenance
DIAGNOSIS: WHAT'S WRONG WITH IT?

45

within the computer, or is a fault of the operator (most common cause of trouble) or within the software (second most common cause of trouble).

The computer will normally tell you exactly what is wrong, and where. The symptoms will indicate what is causing trouble. From there it is a process of elimination until the exact cause has been found.

If you have a diagnostics diskette, go through all the testing procedures provided on the diskette while your system is operating correctly so you will know what things are *supposed* to look like.

Anytime something seems to be malfunctioning, take notes. Make drawings if you do any disassembly. Both will guide you along and will provide valuable information if you have to consult a technician.

A proper diagnostics routine consists of these steps:

1. Check for operator error.
2. Check for software error.
3. Visually check for the obvious.
4. Use built-in self test.
5. Run the diagnostics diskette (if you have one).
6. Be sure to take notes throughout; make drawings when needed.
7. Repair or replace when you can.
8. Consult a technician when you can't, armed with all the above information to save time and money.

46

Chilton's Guide to Macintosh Repair and Maintenance
DIAGNOSIS: WHAT'S WRONG WITH IT?

Chapter 3
Diskettes and Software

If you were to tell a repair technician that your computer was malfunctioning (assuming that the problem wasn't obviously something like a power supply failure), he would immediately try to find out two things. First, what was the operator doing at the time? Second, is the software functioning? (For that matter, has it *ever* functioned?) Many "computer malfunctions" are one of these.

Operator error occurs for many reasons. Even the most experienced operator can make a mistake now and then. The more complex the program is, the more likely it is that the fault is with the operator. Before you write a nasty letter to the software or hardware manufacturer, eliminate all possibility of operator error. (Don't be too surprised if you find that the fault is yours, even if you're sure that it is not.)

Ask yourself, "What have I done wrong?" Then ask, "Has it *ever* worked?" Don't answer either too quickly. After all, would you rather spend hours and hours tearing apart a machine, or a few seconds to be honest with yourself?

Go through the manual and other documentation again. These materials are notorious for being poorly written (I know several people who have erased $500 programs due to confusing instructions in the "Installation" sections of the manuals.) If the software package was produced outside Apple, the people at Apple probably had very little control over what did and did not go into the manual. Many manuals have an index, which can help you find the information you need on a particular subject quickly, even though the information may be scattered through the manual. However, even when an index is present, it may not be accurate.

New programs are always suspect, both for software error and for operator error. If you've never tried to use the program before, you may not be putting in the proper commands. (Back to that lousy manual again.) Or you might be using a feature of the program for the first time. (Back to the manual.)

All clear? The fault is *definitely* not yours but with the diskette? Fine. Now we can proceed.

DISKETTES

The usual method of data input and data storage with the Macintosh is the 3½" diskette. These diskettes are often called *floppies* because they are flexible (inside that case), or, more accurately, *microfloppies*. They are sometimes called simply *media*.

There are actually three completely different types of microfloppies available, designed by Hitachi/Maxell, by Tabor, and by Sony. Only the Sony design (offered by Sony, TDK, Verbatim, and other manufacturers) will work in the Macintosh. (The actual manufacturer doesn't matter as long as the design is correct.)

The Hitachi/Maxell design is similar to that used in the Macintosh in that the diskette is enclosed in a hard plastic case. However, this design is more rectangular and the disk material is slightly smaller in diameter. The Tabor microfloppy has a 3¼" diameter. In appearance it looks just like a smaller version of the 5¼" floppy. Neither will work in the Macintosh. If this isn't obvious in the store where you buy them, it certainly will be if you try to load them into the computer.

If you think about what a diskette is and what it does, it might seem strange that they don't cause even more problems.

Information can really be packed onto the surface of the diskette. Each byte is made up of eight bits (or pulses), yet each byte takes up less than a ten-thousandth of a square inch. Just as your Macintosh won't accept a command with a character missing, it probably won't accept a program with a scratch or blockage, even if the damage is less than a thousandth of an inch in any direction.

Scratches and other damage are minimized by that hard plastic case on the floppy. It also helps to keep the dust out. The metal slide opens only when the the diskette package is inserted into the drive. (It should never be opened manually, except as a last resort to visually inspect the media for damage.)

Diskettes are the least expensive part of your system. They are also one of the most critical. If you try to save money by buying cheap or poor-quality diskettes, you're taking the chance of losing in a larger sense. Although an unknown brand might be of equal quality to those manufactured by the "big name" brands, you are generally better off dealing with a respected brand, at least for critical programs and data. Get the best possible.

HOW DISKETTES ARE MADE

The diskette begins as a thin sheet of flexible plastic. Mylar is the standard. (Mylar is a trademark of Dupont. The generic name for the material is *poly-*

ethylene terephthalate.) The plastic comes to the disk manufacturer in rolls that are about a foot wide and often about a mile in length. The rolls are tested, inspected, and cleaned.

Next the plastic is given a magnetic coating on both sides (even if the diskette is later given the "single sided" label). This coating is made up of extremely fine magnetic particles, a binder (like glue), and a lubricant. The microscopic particles have to be "glued" to make a perfectly uniform coating across the surface of the plastic. If they are not, there will be gaps and data will not be accurately recorded or read.

Next the coated plastic is smoothed and placed back on the roll, and then each roll is given a number for identification so the manufacturer can keep track of it. It is then stamped into the disk shape and is polished (burnished). The rougher the surface is, the more damage it will do to the diskette read/write heads. (The lubricant also reduces head wear.) It isn't possible to get rid of all wear, but efforts to reduce this are made by all the better manufacturers.

The finished diskettes are placed inside the rectangular outer case made of hard plastic. Inside this case is a layer of thin, soft material that helps to keep the surface of the diskette clean. Without this layer the diskette would be constantly "attacking" the read/write head with particles of dust and other contaminants. The liner helps to protect the read/write heads by gently cleaning contaminants away. It also protects the diskette surface by preventing the soft diskette from rubbing against the harder plastic jacket.

Tests are run throughout the manufacture of the diskette. Its final label (single sided, double sided, single density, double density, quad density, etc.) is determined by these testings. A diskette that passes all the tests is given the highest rating and bears the highest price. The more tests the diskette fails, the lower its rating and the lower its price.

What this means in simple terms is that the least expensive diskettes (single sided, single density) have the same basic surface and manufacture. They've just failed some highly sophisticated test along the way and the manufacturer doesn't want to guarantee that the diskette will accurately hold data in higher densities. It's a fairly common practice for computer owners to try to save money by buying the less expensive single sided diskettes and use them as double sided.

ANATOMY OF A DISKETTE

The computer's initializing program divides the diskette into the correct number of tracks and sectors, and it sets the size of those sectors. A diskette formatted by another computer will simply not work in the Macintosh. The formatting routines destroy all data stored on the diskette, so *do not* attempt to format a diskette that has data on it you wish to save.

For the Macintosh there are 80 tracks per side. These are like the grooves of a record, except that they are concentric circles rather than spiral. A

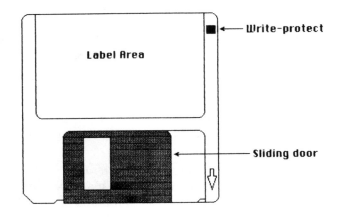

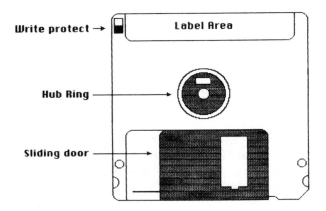

FIG. 3—1 Anatomy of a diskette.

double sided drive will have a total of 160 tracks, arranged in pairs called cylinders. A cylinder is made up of two tracks, one on each side of the diskette in the same relative location. This greatly reduces wear and tear on the drives. It also means that a single-sided drive cannot read a diskette recorded on a double-sided drive. (However, if the diskette was recorded on a single-sided drive, a double-sided drive will have no trouble reading it.)

Each track is further divided into sectors. The number of sectors per track will vary, depending on the tracks being used. The outer 16 tracks (the largest ones physically) have 12 sectors each. Each block of 16 tracks decreases the number of sectors by one. So, the next block of 16 tracks contain 11 sectors each; the next group of 16 will have 10 sectors each; and so on until you reach the inner 16 tracks with 8 sectors per track.

This makes up a total of 800 sectors per side. Each sector is capable of holding 512 bytes of information. By multiplying 800 × 512 you'll get 409,600. To make things easier it is called 400,000, or 400K.

When you hear your disk drive grind it is because the read/write head is moving from track to track. (The sound you hear is the head stepper motor causing the read/write head to move. For more information on this see Chapter 4.) Standard track width is a few thousandths of an inch, with normal density being capable of holding more than 6000 bits per linear inch.

Obviously, if you have double-sided drives, this storage is doubled, with the same specifications for each side of the diskette, but divided into cylinders as mentioned above.

In the center of the diskette is a round metal disk about an inch in diameter. This allows the spindle in the drive to make contact with the diskette and spin it.

At one side is a metal slide. Beneath this is a rectangular opening in the plastic that allows the read/write head of the drive to get at the information. This is the most sensitive part of the entire diskette. A fingerprint here can cause all sorts of troubles, both to the data (including format information) and to the read/write head in the drive.

In one corner of most diskettes is a small notch or hole with a piece of plastic that slides back and forth. This allows a small sensor inside the drive (see Chapter 4) to activate the recording head. A general rule is that when you can see through the square hole, the diskette is protected. The recording head cannot function, and you cannot write information onto the diskette. (You can read from the diskette, however. It's a good habit to protect any diskette that has data you won't be changing.)

The easiest way to be sure is to look at the hole. If you can see through it, the diskette is protected. If you can't see through it, for whatever reason, you can write to the diskette.

One notable exception to this write-protection rule is for diskettes manufactured by Hewlett-Packard. The HP diskettes have a breakaway plastic tab as well as the sliding notch. The idea was to provide a way to more permanently protect a diskette. Snap out the tab and you won't be able to write to the diskette. The error some people make is to remove and discard the plastic tab. This tab can be reinserted to become a sliding write-protect tab. Removing this tab permanently protects the diskette. If you've thrown it away, you won't have the option of unprotecting the diskette in the future. (See the directions that came with the HP diskettes if you have any.)

HOW DELICATE IS A DISKETTE?

Despite its apparent fragility, the diskette is surprisingly tough. Many professional technicians have stories of playing catch with an unjacketed diskette, and then have it perform flawlessly. Diskettes that have been almost shredded by deep scratches zip through the drive as though brand new.

At the same time, a tiny piece of dust can cause a diskette to "crash" and become useless. You're never sure which will happen. Nor is lost data the only risk. Each speck of dust can be ruining the read/write head while it is slowly grinding the magnetic coating from the diskette surface.

The diskettes used by the Macintosh are much tougher than the floppies used by most computers. That hard plastic case protects them extremely well. Even so, things can still happen to them.

The disk drive of the Macintosh reads and writes 80 tracks per side. There are also the empty spaces between the tracks. The recorded data is squeezed into about an inch (which includes the gaps between the tracks). On a normal single-sided drive, the 409,600 bytes per side are packed into about 3 square inches of surface area.

Now you can see why the diskettes and drives are so sensitive. The read/write heads record or retrieve information from tracks that are less than a hundredth of an inch wide and separated from each other by another hundredth of an inch—all this while the diskette is spinning merrily at a speed of between 390 and 605 rpm. If the accuracy is off by just a slight amount, or if something gets in the way, the data on the diskette may be inaccessible.

CARE OF DISKETTES

You can't easily "repair" software. If your business program is malfunctioning, you won't be able to get inside to fix it. (Some programs can be fixed, such as those you've written yourself or those written in a language you can use such as BASIC.) Your goal is to prevent problems before they exist.

Software problems can be greatly reduced by simply taking care of the diskettes. The disk is tough but not indestructible. It's also unpredictable at times. One day you can play catch with the diskette and have it work. The next day a speck of dust or particle of cigarette smoke could fall onto the diskette and wipe out everything. (Not only can you lose software and stored data, you can cause damage to the disk drives by not properly caring for the diskettes.) According to *Verbatim*, at least 80% of all diskette failure is attributable to fingerprints. These are kept to a minimum by the plastic case and metal slide, but there are a surprising number of people who push back the protective slide and touch the diskette material.

One person brought home a brand new, and expensive, program for his Mac. Before he even had the chance to give it a try, his three-year-old son with jam on his fingers pushed back the slide, and . . . . There aren't many manufacturers who will warranty a program against children with peanut butter and jelly.

Other people have the unconscious habit of flicking that metal slide, and then wonder why the diskette has loading problems.

Care of diskettes is not complicated, nor is it time consuming. The manufacturers of the diskette media have taken great pains to ensure that the diskettes will last for a very long time, and with a minimum of problems. Extensive testing is done before the diskettes are sold. Care is also taken to make the diskettes as tough as possible. It's not uncommon to find a manufacturer who guarantees that the diskette will not fail even after several million passes per track. In time this translates to nearly a year of constant running before the life expectancy is reached for a diskette. Since normal operation calls for the diskette to be running just seconds out of every operating hour, the disk should, and could, last a lifetime.

The lifespan of a diskette also depends on how it is used. Although the manufacturer might guarantee the diskette for three million passes per track, each time you use the diskette it goes to the "directory" track. Some applications refer to this same track over and over again. Thus, the life of a diskette depends largely on how many times the one track can be used. As soon as this track wears out, the rest of the diskette is essentially dead.

The diskette can withstand any temperature between 50 and 120°F (10 to 50°C) and still operate without error. Even if the temperature happens to go beyond this range, the diskette is still likely to recover if you give it enough time to cool down or warm up. (See "Heat and Cold" below.)

Humidity does little actual damage. The official range for a diskette is between 20% and 80% (5% to 95% for storage). Drier environments tend to dry out the diskette (although it *does* take quite a while). Worse, static can build up, causing changes in data. More humid areas may cause dust to stick to the diskette. Humidity can also cause the liner to swell. If this happens the diskette may not spin properly and you'll get an error.

CLEANLINESS

When not in use, store all diskettes in their cover jackets and preferably standing vertically inside a box as well. This is to reduce the possibility of contamination by dust and other particles. The soft inner lining will help to protect the read/write heads, but it tends to capture particles which in turn can scratch the diskette. With the data being so tightly packed (409,600 bytes per side), even a small scratch can have devastating effects. That scratch may occur on an unimportant part of the diskette. It might also happen over a critical bit of data and make the rest of the diskette useless.

A quality storage box might cost $30 or more. This sounds expensive until you think of what you're protecting. Many computer owners have hundreds of dollars invested in software, and perhaps thousands of hours

TABLE 3–1.
Diskette Specification Standards

Tracks per side	80
Track width	.006 to .008
Temperature (operation)	50 to 112 F
	10 to 44 C
Temperature (storage)	−40 to 140 F
	−40 to 60 C
Humidity	
(operation)	20% to 80%
(storage)	5% to 95%
Disk speed	390 to 605 rpm

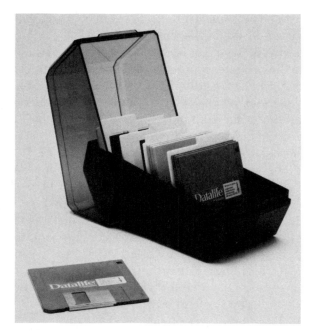

FIG. 3–2 Diskette storage box. Courtesy of International Datawares, Inc.

spent in punching in data. It's not unusual for a computer owner to have more invested in software than in the computer system itself. Why take the chance of throwing all that down the drain just to save a few dollars?

If you can't afford to buy a diskette storage box, make one. Such a box should not be made of metal because of the problem of magnetism. Use wood, plastic, or even cardboard. The inside should be clean and unpainted (fumes). The top should close tightly enough to seal out dust. Beyond that it can be as fancy or as simple as you wish. (I know people who use modified shoe boxes with great success.)

Wood and cardboard boxes are not good solutions, however. Wood and paper both have large amounts of dust and other small particles, no matter how well you clean them. These particles can ruin the diskettes and possibly the drive. Plastic is a much better solution, but it is more difficult to work with. By the time you've bought the plastic and built the case, you probably would have saved by just buying a pre-made box.

An excellent solution for a cheap diskette storage box is to use a plastic freezer container. Due to the small size of the diskettes used by the Macintosh, it's fairly easy to find one that will hold the diskettes nicely. The tops to these containers are often meant to create an airtight seal. This prevents dust from getting in and around the diskettes, and gives you a storage box that is inexpensive and nearly perfect.

However you do it, keep dust, particles, and other contaminants to a minimum. You've invested too much time and money to waste it on a lousy environment.

If a diskette gets dirty, *do not* attempt to clean it. Your cleaning is virtually guaranteed to cause more damage than any amount of dust. How dirty the diskette is and what kind of contamination it has will determine what you do with it. If it isn't too bad, store it for severe emergencies. Otherwise toss it out. A dirty diskette means that it's time to pull out one of the backups. (Make another backup before going to work.)

MAGNETISM

Since the data on the diskettes is stored magnetically, it should be obvious that you have to keep the diskettes away from other sources of magnetism. Yet computer operators are constantly erasing their valuable programs and data by not observing this rule. Some cases are as blatant as setting the diskette next to the magnet of a speaker. Most involve more subtle sources.

Inside the telephone is a small electromagnet. Normally it just sits there and does nothing. Whenever someone calls, however, that little device lets fly with enough magnetism to destroy a diskette. (It rings the bell in the telephone.)

Other potentially dangerous sources are the monitor, the printer, the modem, the cabinet of the computer, any tape recording machine, flourescent lights, and even a calculator. Motors work by using magnetic fields. If you're not sure, don't trust it. (Anything metal is automatically suspect.)

It's unlikely that these subtle sources of magnetism will ruin a program, but why take the chance? It's easier to pay attention to the surroundings and keep the diskettes away from any possible danger.

HEAT AND COLD

Keep the diskettes away from all sources of heat, sun and other. Leaving a diskette in the open sunlight is very likely to cause damage. Even if it's too close to a normal incandescent lamp it could pick up enough heat to cause damage.

At the very least, heat can warp the jacket of the diskette. If this happens, the data you've recorded won't be in the same place on the diskette. It won't matter, though. If the diskette or jacket become warped, the diskette probably won't spin in the drive anyway.

Extreme cold is also hazardous. Not only can extreme cold cause the diskette to crack, it can cause the recorded data to shift in position. A sudden change in temperature from cold to hot can cause other problems as well, such as condensation of moisture. (You wouldn't take your diskettes into the shower with you, would you?)

Even a slight change in temperature, and the contraction or expansion this causes, can cause the tracks to move away from where they are supposed to be. Keep in mind that the tracks are just less than a hundredth of an inch wide, and that each byte of data covers a mere ten-thousandth of a square inch.

BACKUP COPIES

Although it is not strictly maintenance, ALWAYS make backup copies of important programs (if copyable) and data. The cost of diskettes is low considering their value to you. Making backups is the least expensive method there is to protect yourself against software failure. Make at least two backup copies of all software and data diskettes that are important to you. The more important the original is, the more backups you'll want to make. If the data on those backups is no longer important, you can always reformat the diskettes and use them again if you decide later that you don't need that backup copy. In the meantime you'll be protected.

The manufacturer provides a guarantee that the diskette will function without error for a certain period of time, or for a certain number of passes. These guarantees *do not* guarantee the data on the diskettes, however. If a diskette goes bad, the manufacturer will replace it with a new diskette of the same kind, but the data is lost forever, as is the time you spent in punching it in.

There are programs available for making backups of copy-protected software, such as MacSmith and Copy II Mac. These are meant to be used for legitimate purposes only, and not for pirating (stealing) software. Their function is to provide the end user with a way to make backup copies of purchased software that cannot otherwise be copied. Some people prefer to use these programs for routine copying as well. The cost of these programs is small compared to the insurance provided. If your diskette or program goes bad, you'll have a reserve copy on hand.

PROGRAM PROBLEMS

If you're writing your own programs, you're almost bound to make some mistakes. Depending on the program and language you are using, the computer may tell you that you have made a mistake, and could even show you the line(s) where the mistake was made.

If your program doesn't work, accuse yourself before you accuse the computer. Refer to the program language manuals to make sure that the commands you've punched in are correct. If you like programming, take some courses in the subject. Get some books. (Even then be careful. Just because you read it in a book doesn't necessarily mean that the information is accurate.) Learn the most efficient (and the correct) ways to do things.

When it comes to purchased software, you have much less control over what has been done. Many programs are inaccessible for corrections. Unfortunately, so are all too many software companies. It isn't uncommon for a company to have a disclaimer in the package which says in effect, "If the program doesn't function as promised—tough! You bought it, now it's your problem." Other companies support their products, but at an additional cost.

(The old "If you can't understand our poorly written manual, pay us an extra $100 and we'll explain it to you," attitude.)

At other times you might be pleasantly surprised at the response. There are companies that do everything possible to make sure that the end user is happy and satisfied with the program.

When contacting a company about a software malfunction, be fair to them. Begin by doing everything you can to make sure that the error isn't your own. Read the manual carefully and thoroughly. If the problem still hasn't been solved, be as specific as possible in your communication to the company. Give them as many details as possible, including what you've done to correct the problem, and even the version of that piece of software. They can't give much of a response to a vague question such as "It doesn't work. Why?"

Notes of what you've done will be of help to both you and to the company representative. The more information you provide, the quicker will come the solution to the problem. Even jot down the page numbers in the instruction manual so you can readily refer to the proper sections for that particular function.

One of the advantages of working with a local dealer is that you have a quicker access to information. Even if you haven't purchased a training course on a particular piece of software, they'll probably be happy to answer questions for you. Most will replace defective software without any hassle. (Bring your sales receipt! You can't expect them to guarantee a program that you bought from someone else.)

FAILURE TO BOOT

There are a number of reasons why a program will fail to load. The most common reason is a bad diskette. It may also be the fault of the drive, the power supply, the memory or even the keyboard. Usually it is quite easy to find out what is causing the problem. Do one thing at a time, in a process of elimination until you've located the trouble. Don't forget that the whole problem might be a device or program incompatibility (in theory a program for the Macintosh should work on all Macs with the same amount of memory, but this isn't necessarily true), or a copy protect scheme that is causing an apparent (but not real) malfunction.

Eliminate all the obvious things first. Is there any power at all? (If the plug is in the wall and the outlet has been checked and there is still no power, go to "The Power Supply" in Chapter 6.)

Are you using a new program? Has it *ever* worked? Perhaps the diskette you're using is very old and has simply worn out. Try another diskette, one that you know is good. If this one loads you'll know that the fault lies with the software. (Use a diskette that is not critical. Although it is rare, it is possible for the drive to malfunction and write over the top of a diskette, even if it is write-protected.)

Before tearing anything apart, look for the obvious. Is the diskette loading properly, and the drive clamping on the diskette correctly? (If this is the problem, usually the drive spins continually without any apparent effect and "I can't read your diskette" is displayed on the screen.) Are the cables firmly attached to the drives?

A test of the drives involves switching the drives. Some programs allow you to change the default drive, causing the external drive to pretend to be the internal drive. You will probably have to do the job manually. To do this you'll have to open the cabinet and change the way the drives are set up by swapping the connectors. Detailed information on how to go about this is provided in Chapter 4.

You'll know quickly if the malfunction is in a drive or elsewhere. If drive A was refusing to load, and still refuses to load when configured as drive B, chances are good that the drive is at fault. If the drive swap doesn't change things, the problem is elsewhere. (See Chapter 4.)

OTHER PROBLEMS

There will be times when a program loads and operates normally, only to malfunction while the program is running. Data may suddenly come out changed, or missing. The program could lock up the keyboard, causing the loss of the data you've been punching in.

If the problem is in the software (in the program itself), you should be able to reproduce the malfunction by pressing the same keys again. You may have already noticed where the failure occurs. (Don't forget to check the manual and eliminate the possibility of operator error!) Notes will come in very handy in tracking down the problem.

Changed or garbled data can often be the result of overediting. The computer will automatically assign a chunk of data to a spot on the diskette. If possible it will record these chunks in sequence. If something else has been placed in the next open spot on the diskette, the data will be moved along until an open spot is found. This tends to break the file up all over the diskette. In reading such a broken file the computer might miss something.

The solution for this is to copy files occasionally. This will help to rearrange the file in sequential order. You can make a copy of a single file or the entire disk.

For copying just one file, you have the choice of duplicating it on the same disk under a different name, or on another disk. The first choice is fine. The second choice is even better since it puts the information on a completely different diskette. If something happens to your main diskette, the backup will be holding the same data.

It is best to use a freshly formatted diskette for the copy, since a diskette with data on it could break up the files even more (to make it fit between the existing files).

One part of the diskette is set aside for "File Allocation." Each time you bring up the directory of the diskette, the computer goes to this track and displays the files. Each time you tell the computer to load in a program or data file, it again goes to the allocation table to find out where the needed file is.

Earlier in this chapter we talked about how many passes a diskette can withstand before malfunction (three million passes per track). This seems as though the diskette could indeed last forever. It *will* last for many years. The main reason it wears out is due to the passes against the directory. Each time the file is read, recorded, or used in any way, the drive head goes back to the allocation track. After heavy use, this track might fail. Even though the information is still good on the rest of the diskette, it is difficult to get at it because the allocation area no longer tells the computer where to look.

This same track can become faulty for other reasons. Some programs do not "exit gracefully." If the program is in use and you lose power—by shutting down or through a power outage—the allocation table can become messed up. The end result is about the same as if the track had worn out.

The solution for both is prevention. Make backup copies of everything important. The more you use a particular diskette, the more important backups are. If a diskette has been in use for a long time, make a copy and replace it *before* it gives out.

SUMMARY

Most computer malfunctions are caused by either the operator or by the software. Eliminating operator error is a matter of proper training and paying attention. The simplest beginning is to read the instructions. Learn how to work with the program and how to handle its functions and its quirks.

Since you are unlikely to be the author of your functional programs, you cannot eliminate software problems. If the package comes to you with flaws in it, there won't be much that you can do, other than to return the package for a refund. As soon as possible after getting a new program, test it out. The longer you wait to do this, the more difficult it will be to get a refund or an exchange.

Make backups of all important software and data diskettes. Two backup copies of each is none too few. It's an inexpensive insurance against loss through operator goof-up, diskette flaw, or drive malfunction.

Taking care of the diskettes is a simple matter of preventive maintenance. Provide a clean environment. Keep the diskettes away from things that could damage them, such as magnetism, heat, contaminants, and physical dangers.

Handle diskettes properly and they can last a lifetime. When they finally wear out, you always have the backup copies to turn to.

Chapter 4
The Disk Drives

The electronics of a computer allows electrons to move through the proper components at the proper times. The only motion is that of the electrons, and virtually the only wear is that caused by heating and cooling. Something mechanical is bound to have more troubles than something that doesn't move physically at all.

The only mechanical parts of the Macintosh are the printer and the disk drives. (The keyboard is sometimes considered to be mechanical in that it requires a physical movement of the keys to operate.) Of all failures in your computer system, most will involve either the printer or the drives. (Printers are covered in Chapter 6.)

The disk drives are critical parts of the computer system. There isn't much that your computer can do without them.

The key is prevention. Read Chapters 3 and 7 and follow the maintenance information, and you'll have far fewer problems. When something *does* go wrong, this chapter can help you find the problem. If you can't fix the existing drive, turn to Chapter 8 for information on how to replace a disk drive.

THE BASICS

The drive itself is tucked inside a metal shield that usually has to be removed before you can do much to the drive. On the top of the drive is the analog card. This is the main circuitry of the drive. The top board is linked with a second board on the bottom. This second board contains the servo circuits. This circuitry works together with the main digital board of the computer to control the mechanical parts of the drive, such as drive speed, head movement, and so forth.

The chip on the motherboard responsible for disk drive control is a custom chip designed by Apple. It is located by the two ROM chips (also

FIG. 4-1 Inside the Macintosh, showing the disk drive. Note the metal shield around the drive and the flat ribbon cable coming to the drive from the main digital board.

custom chips) on the main digital circuit board, and it has an IWM on the board next to the chip. IWM stands for "integrated Woz machine," after Steve Wozniak, the person responsible for the design of the chip. (For more information on this chip, see "Testing the Drive Controller Chip" below.)

You can perform certain tests to determine if these boards are causing a malfunction. Most of the time it doesn't matter since repair is by replacement of the entire drive. The drives are not meant to be repaired. Finding the boards alone, or any disk drive parts for that matter, is difficult at best and is usually impossible. In most cases, all you can do is to save money by performing the actual replacement yourself.

It's a good idea to check around in your area to see if individual parts are available before you spend a lot of time diagnosing. A look at your drives should give you a fair idea if you want to continue diagnosis, or if you will stop at finding the faulty drive as a whole. For most people, a complete replacement will be the usual, and preferred, route.

CHECK THE OBVIOUS

Serious malfunctions in the drive are relatively rare. Most of the problems are brought on by small things, and often by things that have nothing to do with drive operation directly. Don't yank out the drives and tear them apart until you've eliminated all the easy things.

FIG. 4–2 Location of the IWM disk drive controller.

The first place to start is with yourself. Are you doing something silly (but surprisingly common) such as putting in the wrong diskette, or even the right diskette but upside down? If you're starting up the computer, does the diskette you're trying to use have the operating system on it?

Next, try different software. The diskette you are attempting to load could be faulty. A faulty diskette is more likely than a faulty drive. (See Chapter 3 for more information on software and software problems.) You may also be trying to use one of the programs that is meant for a Macintosh with more memory in it. Try a different program, one that you know has worked before.

If you haven't cleaned the heads in some time, there could be deposits that are preventing the heads from operating. False or intermittent data read/write could mean that a dirty head is causing a problem. (See Chapter 7 for more information on cleaning the drive heads.)

Have you made any changes in your system? If so, you may have changed the way the computer "looks" at the world around it, including the drives. If everything was working perfectly before the change, you've probably done something wrong in making the change.

If cabling was necessary in making the addition, have you used the correct kind of cable, with the correct pin allocations? Chapter 8 gives you a listing of the various I/O (input/output) ports of your computer. These, plus the information provided in the instruction manual that came with the peripheral, will help you to match everything correctly. It may seem strange to have the drives appear to be malfunctioning due to a printer connection, but it can happen.

It's also important that the cables are plugged in correctly. The connectors are keyed, which makes it virtually impossible to make a mistake. (This may not be true with some peripherals.) Still, it is important to look at the way the cable is plugged in. Make a sketch of the proper alignment of the cable and connector if you're in doubt. If the cable doesn't plug in easily, don't force it.

Are the cables and connectors secure? Try unplugging them and push-

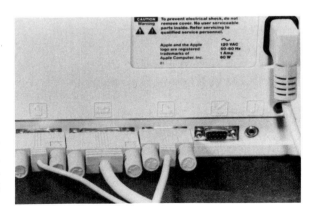

FIG. 4–3 Check the connectors, both as they fit on the components and for good contact between the wiring at the connector.

FIG. 4—4 Location of the disk drive signal cable on the main board. Be very careful when cleaning pin-type contacts.

ing them back into place (with the power off!). If the contacts appear to be a little dirty, clean them. Use a cleaner that doesn't leave a residue. Cleaning pin-type contacts requires a little more care, but if you use a quality cleaning fluid only, you'll have no problems. Be sure to shut down the power before removing or inserting any cables or circuit boards. Failure to do so will almost certainly damage the board and the computer.

OBSERVE SYMPTOMS

Before you go into the actual diagnostics to find out what has gone wrong with a drive, you can try several easy things.

The first step is *always* to observe the symptoms and then to eliminate those things that are *not* causing the problem. Make a note of all errors.

Are programs able to load at all, even in part? Listen to the sound of the stepper motor. Is it trying to move across the tracks, or is it "stuck" somewhere? Does this happen with all programs you try to load, or just with one?

Are other functions working? If you can't write to a diskette or copy a file, can you format a diskette?

If the internal drive refuses to operate correctly, change the default and try to load the program with the external drive (if you have one), or follow the instructions below and do a drive swap. This means that you'll have to open the cabinet and reconnect the drives so that the external drive operates as the internal drive, and vice versa.

Try to boot the operating system diskette. You're now loading only the system, and not a full program. (See Chapter 3, "Failure to Boot.")

Check all cable and board connections, and clean them if they appear to be dirty. When was the last time you cleaned the heads?

Try to eliminate all the obvious things before you spend a lot of time and effort. Chances are good that you'll find that the problem isn't really a problem at all.

THE CLAMPING MECHANISM

As you insert the diskette the clamping mechanism goes down and the diskette is placed in the correct position for the spindle to make a positive contact and for the read/write head to be positioned to do its job. If the clamping mechanism doesn't come down and lock into place properly, the computer is likely to think the drive is empty. The diskette can't spin, the program can't load.

The usual result of a malfunctioning clamping mechanism is that the computer will wait for you to insert a disk, which you won't be able to do to the satisfaction of the computer. The problem could also be intermittent, with data being read or recorded with errors.

The clamping mechanism is made of plastic and thin metal. Some have the unfortunate tendency to break or bend. Even if the break hasn't completely disabled the drive, it could still prevent the drive from functioning properly. The hub may not make a secure contact with the diskette or the drive may simply think that it's empty.

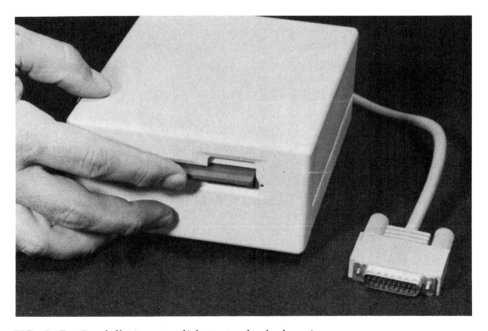

FIG. 4—5 Carefully insert a diskette to check clamping.

FIG. 4—6 Lubricating the mechanisms might help, but this is a last resort and must be done carefully.

Adjusting or repairing this mechanism is difficult. In most cases, the only thing you can do (and that only if you're *very* careful) is to lubricate the mechanical parts of the mechanism. Even then, it is a last resort before you throw the drive away. There are some dangers involved. (Before you waste your time doing this, visually inspect the mechanism and try to find any obvious binding or other damage.)

The primary danger in lubricating the drive mechanism is that oil doesn't get along at all well with the floppies or the read/write heads. The tiniest bit of contamination will ruin the drive and destroy any diskettes placed into it. Silicon based lubricants are okay. Fine grade machine oil is a little better. Do not use automotive motor oil. Electronics supply houses sell needle-tipped oilers. Even these put out too much lubricant for the drive. They're meant more for oiling delicate motors through access holes.

To lubricate the mechanisms of the drive, use a swab with a very tight tip. (You don't want the threads to flake off.) Put a drop of oil on the tip of this, and gently apply the oil that way. Then work the mechanism by hand several times until it operates freely again. Most of the time you'll be able to see where the lubricate has been placed at the factory.

EJECTION PROBLEMS

Ejecting a diskette is done either by selecting the Eject command on the screen or by holding down the Command key (the key with the little

FIG. 4–7 The manual eject hole is next to the diskette slot.

"flower" to the left of the space bar) and typing the letter "e" (for "eject"). Occasionally, a diskette will refuse to eject normally.

First, check to be sure that you've closed any working files on the diskette to be ejected. Then try the normal Eject command again. It's possible that you made a mistake in entering the command. If this doesn't work, hold down the button on the mouse and turn the computer off and then on again. Do this at least twice before giving up.

As a last resort, you can manually eject the diskette by inserting a stiff wire into the small hole next to the diskette slot. You can use a straightened paper clip or anything else that won't bend or break.

If you have to do it this way, be very careful. And, once you have the diskette out, try the whole thing again. If you have manually ejected that same diskette again, try another diskette. If this one hangs up, too, you probably have a more serious problem—probably with the clamping and ejection mechanism of the drive.

Keep in mind at all times that this mechanism is extremely delicate. Move slowly and cautiously.

CHECKING INCOMING POWER

If the LEDs inside the drive come on (difficult to see, but look closely through the slot), you might assume that power is getting to the drive and eliminate the power supply as the source of the problem. Chances are good that this assumption is valid. There is a simple check to make sure.

Power to the disk drive comes through the signal cable, via pins 9, 11, 13, 15, 17, and 19. Disconnecting the signal cable from the drive makes probing the incoming power easy. Better yet is to test for power on the set of

FIG. 4–8 Disk drive connector.

solder points on the drive analog board, located just above the connector. If you look carefully, you'll see marked on the board which pin is which.

If you get readings within about a half volt of the stated value (4.5 to 5.5 across the 5-volt pins; 11 to 13 across the 12-volt pins), the power supply is kicking out the proper voltages as far as the drives are concerned. And, if power is getting *to* the suspected drive but that drive is dead, chances are good that it is the fault of the drive.

Don't forget to take notes and make sketches. This is especially important if you are going to be doing disassembly, but it is still an essential step to help you keep track of what you're doing, and what you've already done.

Testing power to an external drive is much the same as testing power to the internal drive. See Fig. 4–12 for the pin allocations and correct voltage

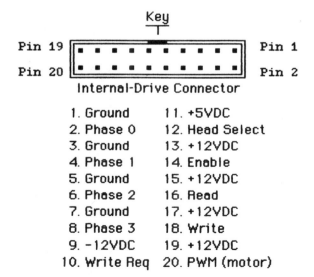

Top View

Key

Pin 19   Pin 1
Pin 20   Pin 2

Internal-Drive Connector

1. Ground	11. +5VDC
2. Phase 0	12. Head Select
3. Ground	13. +12VDC
4. Phase 1	14. Enable
5. Ground	15. +12VDC
6. Phase 2	16. Read
7. Ground	17. +12VDC
8. Phase 3	18. Write
9. -12VDC	19. +12VDC
10. Write Req	20. PWM (motor)

FIG. 4–9 Disk drive signal cable pin allocations.

FIG. 4–10 You can test for power at the drive or at the connector itself.

FIG. 4–11 The external drive connector.

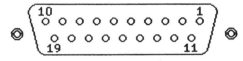

External Disk Connector

1. Ground	11. Phase 0
2. Ground	12. Phase 1
3. Ground	13. Phase 2
4. Ground	14. Phase 3
5. -12VDC	15. Write Req
6. +5VDC	16. Head Select
7. +12VDC	17. Enable
8. +12VDC	18. Read
9. NC	19. Write
10. PWM (motor)	

FIG. 4–12 External drive connector pin allocations.

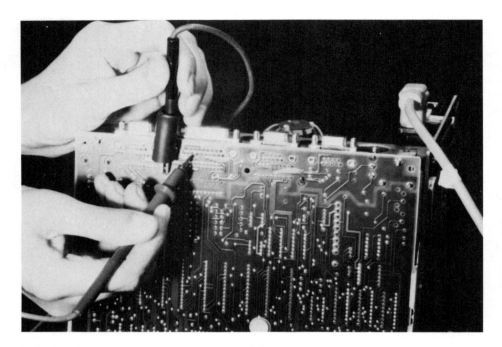

FIG. 4—13 Testing power to an external drive.

readings. You can probe in any of four places. In order of preference: (1) at the main digital board solder joints; (2) at the pins of the external drive connector attached to the main digital board; (3) at the end of the external drive cable after it has been disconnected from the external drive; (4) at the end of the external drive cable while it is still connected.

TESTING THE SIGNAL CABLE

The main signal cable is the flat multi-wired cable that connects the drive to the main board. It attaches to the main board on the left rear by the drives

FIG. 4—14 Routing of the signal cable.

FIG. 4–15 Close-up of the cable connector on the disk drive.

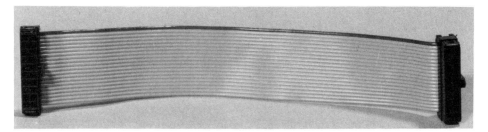

FIG. 4–16 The disconnected main signal cable.

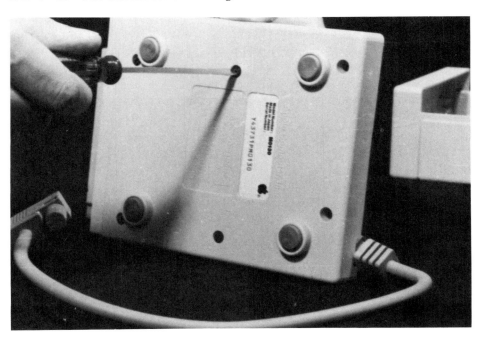

FIG. 4–17 Carefully remove the screws holding together the case of the external drive.

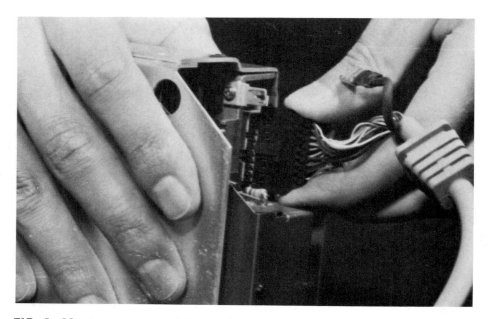

FIG. 4—18 Even more carefully, unplug the cable.

and is the only cable of its type in the computer. It's rare for this cable to go bad, but it is possible. Testing it is easy.

Set your meter to read ohms (resistance). The setting used doesn't matter. Disconnect the cable from both ends. Then, one pair of pins at a time, touch one probe to a pin on one side of the cable, and the other probe to the same pin on the opposite side of the cable. A reading of zero ohms means that the wire between those two pins is good. A reading of infinite ohms (no

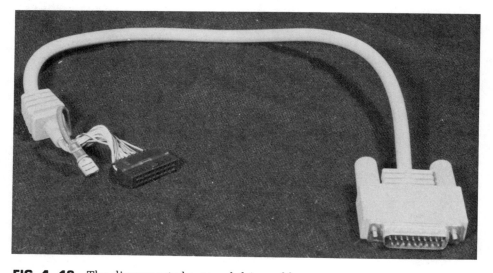

FIG. 4—19 The disconnected external drive cable.

movement of the meter needle) means that the wire is broken somewhere along the cable. (For those interested, this is called checking for continuity, and it is the best way to test *any* wire or cable that is not presently carrying a current. You can even do this to test the wiring between your stereo and speakers.)

Testing the cable to the external drive is much the same. First you'll have to disassemble the external drive so you can get at the cable and connector. Detailed instructions for this are given in the next step ("Drive Swap").

Usual repair is to replace the cable.

DRIVE SWAP

Next, and if you have two floppy drives, you can try a swap. This isn't easy to do, and requires that you open the cabinets of both the computer and the external drive. The time required might be worth it, though. This will almost certainly show you if a particular drive is bad.

Remove the computer cabinet and locate the connector for the internal drive. With the power off, disconnect the plug from the drive and carefully flop it towards the back of the computer.

Carefully remove the cabinet from the external drive. There are six screws on the bottom of the case. Two of these are of the self-tapping variety,

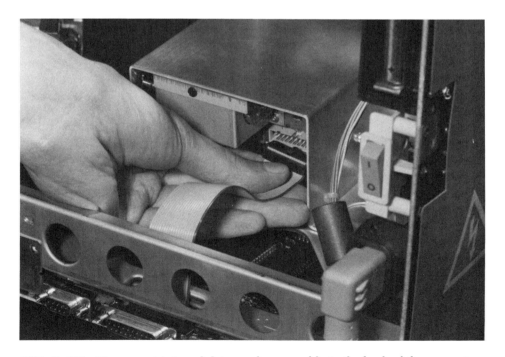

FIG. 4–20 Disconnect internal drive and move cable to the back of the computer.

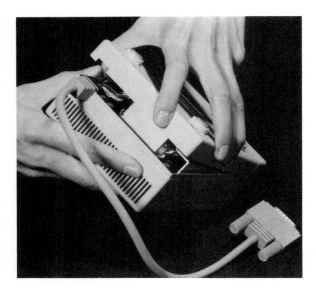

FIG. 4—21 Remove external drive case.

and come to a point. Keep track of where you got these (the two holes in the back). Although it makes no difference which order you use to remove the screws, in putting it all back together again, it's easiest to install these two screws last.

The case comes apart by sliding the cover back slightly to release the lip. Now unplug the two connectors from this drive's analog card—the main signal cable and the grounding lug.

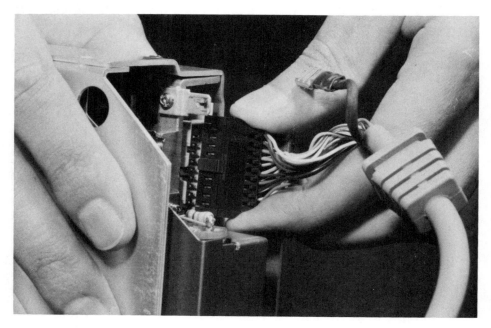

FIG. 4—22 Completely remove the cable, including the ground clip.

Very carefully hold the external drive near the back of the computer and plug in the main connector. It's easiest to do this with the external drive held upside down, which does not affect the performance of the drive. *Do not* let the metal shield of the drive touch anything or you could cause serious damage. The connector only fits one way (it's keyed), so if it doesn't slide on fairly easily, be sure that you have it situated correctly. It's supposed to be snug, but don't force it.

The external drive is now acting as the main, internal drive. If the failure you had previously remains the same, the problem is not with the drive, but with the main digital board (particularly the IWM chip), or possibly the power supply.

TESTING THE DRIVE CONTROLLER CHIP

The floppy drives are controlled by a chip and some related circuitry on the main board. Regardless of the model you have, this chip is some version of the IWM (integrated Woz machine) IC, which is a chip specially designed and manufactured for Apple. You will not be able to find this chip in any electronics supply store.

Unfortunately, the easiest way to test this chip is by replacement with one that is known to be good. Drive problems that are shown to be not in the drives themselves could be solved by changing this one chip—*if* you can find one. Even then, this is a gamble. If you know that the driver chip has failed, replacing it is less expensive than replacing the entire main board. (If this *isn't* the trouble, and you end up changing the main board, if possible keep the old main board on hand for future use. However, keep in mind that the old board normally has a trade-in value.)

Also, the only time you can safely test the chip by swapping it is if the chip is socketed, which is something you just won't see unless someone has gone in and made that specific modification. If it is soldered into place, which is normal, leave it alone. Trying to desolder those 28 pins and soldering in the 28 new ones can only lead to trouble.

Testing the chip with a meter won't tell you much. The chip is an intricate part of the computer's circuitry. The testing is also risky. Power has to be flowing for you to make the test. If your hand slips, if you cause a short circuit, or touch the wrong pins, you won't have to wonder if the chip is bad. You can also cause damage to other parts of the circuit board.

It's best to leave the chip alone, or to leave the testing (and even the swapping) to the technician.

TESTING THE WRITE-PROTECT SENSOR

The notch with the plastic tab on the right rear of the diskette is there to activate (or deactivate) the write-protect sensor inside the drive. With the hole closed, you can write data on the diskette and can erase what is there.

FIG. 4—23 Location of the IWM drive controller chip.

FIG. 4–24 The diskette with the hole open, which protects (hopefully) the data on the diskette.

With the hole open, you cannot change the data on the diskette. However, if the sensor goes bad, the data and programs on the diskettes may be erased. If the drive malfunctions while the write-protect sensor is faulty, you could find yourself with nothing but a blank diskette, even if all you've done is insert the diskette and apply the power. If you find that this sensor is faulty, *do not* attempt to use the disk drive until you have made the repair.

If you suspect that the write-protect circuitry is faulty, and even as an occasional safety check, you can perform a very simple test. Take a diskette that has nothing of value on it. Open the write-protect hole. Then try to write onto the diskette or try to erase it. If the sensor is functioning properly, you won't be able to erase or change anything on the diskette.

SOME OTHER PRECAUTIONS

You can avoid many drive problems simply by prevention. Keep the environment as clean as possible. Dust and other contaminants can create havoc with the drive.

Regular cleaning of the read/write heads is a good practice. How often you do this will depend on your surroundings and how much the computer is used. *Don't skimp* when you are buying a head cleaning kit. Get the best possible. (More information on regular cleaning and maintenance appears in Chapter 7.)

STOP! Don't do anything to your drive until you've made copies of all data that was recorded on the maladjusted drive!

If your drive has to be realigned, or if the drive speed is to be adjusted, make new copies of everything that has been recorded in that drive. Do this *before* you make the adjustments. Use that drive as the "source," with a drive that you know is good for the "target."

The reason for this is that the faulty drive has recorded the data according to its maladjusted characteristics. If you try to read that data on a properly operating drive, you'll probably get nothing but garbage. By using the faulty drive as the "source," you're allowing it to read the data with the characteristics embedded. The good "target" drive will record the data the way it should be.

The Macintosh is designed to be portable. The drives themselves, both floppy and hard, are not. Whenever you move the computer from place to place, protect yourself and the drive heads by inserting either a blank diskette, such as an old one that has gone bad and that you can afford to ruin, or a cardboard drive head protection card (two such cards is better yet).

Most hard drives have a "Move" setting to lock down the read/write head. If you plan to move the hard drive, learn how to operate this feature (if it's not already automatic), and make use of it. Not only can you damage the hard drive, you also stand to lose all the data stored on it.

Earlier in this chapter it was mentioned that you might be able to "fix" a faulty latching mechanism by careful lubrication. The same is true for other mechanical parts of the drive. The same rules apply—namely, *extreme* cau-

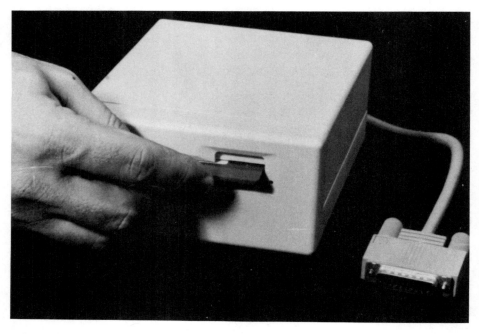

FIG. 4—25 When moving your computer more than a few feet, it's a good idea to insert one or two head protection cards, or a blank diskette.

FIG. 4–26 Any lubrication of the drive, such as on the eject mechanism, must be done carefully—and preferably not at all.

tion and very little lubricant. Lubricating the mechanism must be your last ditch effort before throwing away the drive. Even then, don't use any valuable diskettes in the drive until you are absolutely certain that you haven't contaminated the heads.

REMOVING THE DRIVE

Getting the drive out of your Macintosh can be time-consuming and complicated. First, it requires that you open the cabinet. Then, since the entire computer is self-contained, the inside is prone to stray RF radiation (especially from the video section of your computer). To prevent this from damaging the drive and the diskettes, the drive is encased in a grounded shield.

With the cabinet off, disconnect and then slide out the main digital board. (See Chapter 5 for more details on removing the main board if you are uncertain.) Now you can access the mounting screws that hold the shield to the chassis and the screws that hold the drive to the shield. With the holding screws removed, and all wires and cables disconnected, the drive should slide out of the casing without difficulty. Be very careful doing this.

Follow the reverse procedure to replace the drive.

HARD DRIVES

The floppy disk of the Macintosh can hold up to 400K per side. Using the old standard of 6 characters per word as an average, that works out to be about

FIG. 4—27 The inside of the Macintosh. Note the drive shield casing.

67,000 words. This is accomplished by using a variable speed for the disk rotation in order to make use of every bit of sector space.

A hard drive can hold even more information: 5 and 10 megabyte (millions of bytes) are standard for hard drive. Capacities of 20 megabytes and more aren't uncommon.

The speed at which a diskette can spin is limited. The read/write head comes into physical contact with the diskette. At high speeds this can cause some severe problems. The tiniest piece of dust could destroy both the read/write head and the floppy at high speeds. Friction alone would make the unit inoperable.

The solution is to have the head float along above the disk, without making any actual contact. This basically takes care of itself as the platter of the hard drive spins. The platter spins so quickly that a layer of air is created between the platter and the head. The head floats along, just above the surface of the enclosed disk (by a few millionths of an inch). This just isn't possible with a floppy. The flexible nature of a floppy would cause the distance between a floating read/write head and the diskette to vary too much.

To maintain a uniform distance, the disk itself is solid, or hard. This assures that the distance between the head and the media is constant.

FIG. 4—28 Slide out the main digital board.

FIG. 4—29 Remove the holding screws.

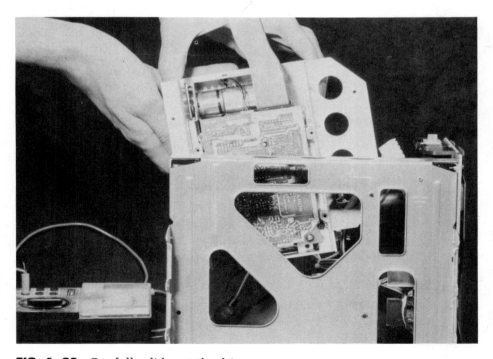

FIG. 4—30 Carefully slide out the drive.

That gap is generally between 10 and 20 millionths of an inch. Not much space, and not much room for errors. A tiny fleck of dust can cause a head crash. This is a literal description of what can happen. The head crashes into the dust particle, or whatever else is in the way, and trouble results. This is why the hard drive is assembled in a special dust-free room, and why you should *never* attempt to open the drive.

Another kind of head crash can result if the head comes down and strikes the media. Crashing into a piece of dust is bad enough. Crashing into the media, especially while the platter is spinning, is almost a guarantee of extensive damage.

And when the hard drive goes down, it takes with it an incredible amount of recorded data. (The solution should be obvious. *Make backups!*)

There are several advantages in owning a hard drive. Most programs and the general operation of the computer will be considerably faster. The typical rate of data transfer for a floppy is around 500,000 bits per second. A hard drive can transfer data ten times faster, or 5,000,000 bits per second. Some hard drives operate at even higher speeds.

This can cause a problem with the Macintosh. You can't use just any hard drive. The data transfer rate of the Macintosh is listed as one megabit (1,000,000 bits) per second, which means that the hard drive is trying to take or supply data five times faster than the Mac can handle. To make matters worse, the actual effective rate of data transfer of the Macintosh is more like 750 kilobits per second.

That rate is just fine for use with floppies, and even has a comfortable margin of safety—that is, the 750 kilobit transfer rate is on the slow side.

The upshot of all this is that if you get a new hard drive, install it correctly, and it fails to work, it could be that there is really nothing wrong but a mismatch in speed. (See Chapter 8 for more details on installation of a hard drive and information on the AppleBus.)

Even if the hard drive has been working, and then suddenly stops, the problem could be with the transfer bus, the controller of the hard drive (often a 68008, such as is used in the Tecmar drive, or a related chip).

Many hard drives have an anti-static button somewhere on the unit. Due to its nature, this button tends to collect dust. If it gets too dirty, you may begin to experience errors or even a complete failure. You can clean this button with a tissue (carefully, and with the power off!).

An additional problem that can come up is a software failure. The Macintosh cannot boot from the hard drive, except for the special internally mounted hard drive made by General Computer Company, called "HyperDrive." A separate program must be inserted into the diskette drive that directs the computer to the hard drive. (This program generally comes with the hard drive when your purchase it.)

If this program fails, most of the time you'll see the sad face icon, signifying that the program did not load. With or without this icon, checking the software is the quickest and easiest first test. Use a backup copy of the

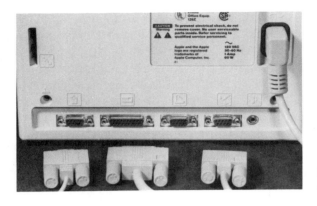

FIG. 4—31 Check the obvious, such as the connectors.

loading program and try again. (You made a backup copy of the program—before even plugging in the hard drive, right?)

Some hard drives do not have a power light or LED, and the only way you can tell if they are working at all is if you lean close and listen. When power is applied, you should be able to hear the drive coming up to the proper speed. This coming up to speed takes a little time. While this is taking place, the hard drive program will be loading into the computer. Normally, a special hard drive icon will appear on the screen, or some other signal will appear indicating that something is happening. To know for sure, the only way is to become familiar with the peculiarities of your hard drive, prefera-

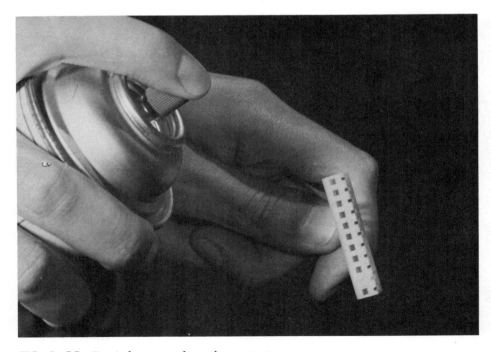

FIG. 4—32 Don't forget to clean the contacts.

bly before you attempt to install the unit. (Ask the dealer what to expect. *And read the manual!*)

Not much can be done about repair or maintenance of a hard drive. The unit is sealed at the factory. Any internal repairs must be done in a special, dust-free atmosphere. It simply cannot be done at home.

Your efforts at repair and maintenance will have to be confined to cleaning the contacts and static eliminator, reseating the chips, and checking the connectors. Anything more complex than this should be left to a professional—one who is willing to guarantee in writing that any damage caused by carelessness or incorrect procedure will be covered. Really about all you can do about a hard drive problem is to replace the unit, or bring your computer to the shop.

SUMMARY

The disk drives are probably the most critical part of your computer system. Unfortunately, they are also the devices most likely to cause troubles. This is because they are one of the few mechanical parts in the system.

If the drive malfunctions, existing programs may not operate. Data recorded on a faulty drive can disappear once the drive is put back into shape again.

Only rarely will a drive suddenly fail. Most of the time it will give you warning symptoms, such as a faulty read or a faulty write. Both can be caused by other things, but both also indicate that it is time to check out the drives.

Make drive checks and drive maintenance a part of your regular schedule. Clean the heads occasionally. A diagnostics diskette is a good investment. Run the diagnostics on the drives regularly to keep track of how the drives are performing. This way you'll have ample warning if the drive is going bad.

Preventive maintenance is the best possible means of assuring that the drives will give you no problems. Backup copies of programs and data diskettes made while the drives are operating properly will help to ensure that a drive malfunction is not a disaster.

When you have finished the tests in this chapter, or by simply taking note of the symptoms, you'll have a very good idea as to where the problem is. If power is getting to the drives from the power supply, the problem is most likely with the drive or cable. A simple continuity test eliminates the cable as the possible cause.

Hard drives present a special problem. Their construction makes it impossible for you to work on them other than to check for some of the very simple and obvious things. Never attempt to disassemble the hard drive.

Chapter 5
Troubleshooting the Boards

The Macintosh makes use of only two boards inside. One is the analog board, which supplies power to everything in the computer and holds the video circuitry. The other is the digital board, more commonly, and incorrectly, called the motherboard.

There are many things on the circuit boards that cannot be tested without some very expensive equipment. Much of the time the diagnostic steps you take will do no more than to let you know which board is malfunctioning. Only rarely will you be able to track the problem to a specific component. About the only time you'll be able to find the specific component that is causing the problem is when there is obvious damage. Repair is usually by replacement of the entire board.

The professional in a repair shop has an advantage. If the analog board is suspected, for example, they are likely to have another one close at hand. This can be substituted for the suspected board. If things work again, the problem has been found and the repair is complete. If this doesn't solve the problem, there aren't many more things left to swap before the real problem is discovered.

The same technique can be used for individual components, and once again the shop has the advantage of having a stock of components on hand. If the suspected component is socketed, the swap takes just a few seconds.

Unfortunately, neither avenue is open to the average end user. The cost of keeping all the spares on hand would be much higher than paying the shop. You'll almost certainly have to limit yourself to tracking the malfunction to a board rather than to a component.

More important than any tests you can perform is careful observation. Look for symptoms. What is happening? What is not happening that should be? Then look for the obvious. Are all the connectors plugged in correctly? If you're one of the lucky ones who has a board with socketed components, give each and everyone a push to make certain that they are seated in the sockets. (Don't fiddle with any connectors or components while the power is flowing.)

You should have a good idea of which board is causing the problem after you've completed your observation survey. By process of elimination, you should be able to locate what could be causing the problem—and not waste time on things that can't be causing it. Before you begin any testing or measurement, you should already have a good idea that the board you are testing is the cause of the malfunction. Chances are you won't have to make any actual tests other than for power.

THE MAIN DIGITAL BOARD

The term "motherboard" is used by Apple to describe the main circuit board of their II series computers; "digital board" as the correct term for the main circuit board of the Macintosh. IBM calls theirs a "system board." Other companies use other names, such as "main board." Whatever you call it, it's essentially the same thing.

Unfortunately, if something is wrong with the digital board, you probably won't be able to do much about it other than to swap it with a new one, or take it to an experienced technician who has the right test equipment. Expect him to just replace the entire board. Even if the problem *can* be tracked to a single component, the labor charges involved with this lengthy search can cost you more than the new board.

If you're lucky, the service personnel might be able to guess at the cause of the problem by the symptoms you describe. Once again, it's important to take notes. The shop may then be able to swap individual components (such

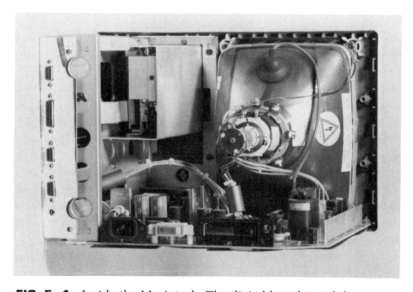

FIG. 5–1 Inside the Macintosh. The digital board is at left.

FIG. 5–2 A typical recent main digital board.

as socketed ICs) with known good ones in their stock. This route to finding the problem isn't open to the average owner, though, since not many of us keep a shelf full of computer parts.

Most Macintosh main boards have virtually all components soldered into place. This means that a problem with the RAM chips, for example, requires that the end user or shop has to spend some frustrating time trying to desolder the multipinned ICs (16 pins per chip, with 8 chips in the RAM section of the main board), and then solder in the new chips. The usual solution is to avoid all this and replace the entire circuit board.

Some main boards have more socketed components, which makes a simple swap considerably easier. Generally, if your main board has sockets other than the two for the ROM, someone has modified it (such as during a RAM upgrade to a 128K machine).

The malfunctioning board has a trade-in value. If you damage the board in some way, such as burning it with a soldering iron while attempting to change a chip, this trade-in value disappears. If you decide to attempt any repairs, do so with extreme caution. The same applies for any modifications to the hardware you might decide to make.

TEST THE POWER SUPPLY FIRST

Before you yank out the digital board and pay for a new one, try to determine if the board is actually at fault. As mentioned, this isn't easy. Tests made with a VOM, or even with an oscilloscope, aren't necessarily conclusive. They are just indicators.

Shut off the power and check the system board carefully to be sure that all connectors are secure. Unplug them and inspect the contacts for signs of burning or corrosion. Cleaning them might not take care of a problem, but it is such a quick and easy process that you might as well give it a try. Clean the contacts (the pins or "fingers") with a quality cleaner. *Do not* use a cleaner that has any kind of residue in it. Television tuner cleaner, for example, has a lubricant in it and will cause more problems than it will cure.

Some peripherals use flat connectors along board edges, usually like rectangles of solder along a board edge. These can be cleaned with the same

FIG. 5–3 The "heart" of the digital board—the 68000 CPU on the left, and the two ROM chips and IWM disk drive controller in the middle.

FIG. 5—4 Digital board with the main parts labelled.

spray cleaner used on pin contacts. If you're careful, they can also be cleaned with a soft eraser, such as those found on many pencils. Do this cleaning away from the device to avoid getting the eraser crumbs into the machine.

With the power still off, gently press down on all socketed ICs to make sure that they are in good contact with their sockets. This is especially important if the computer or peripheral has been moved around.

While you're going through these steps, visually inspect everything inside the computer. You might be able to spot a damaged component or something else that is obviously at fault. Now try the system again.

If things still don't function properly, get out your meter and set it to read 12 volts DC. You'll be testing the power flowing into the main board by measuring across pins of the 10-pin power supply connector. This is located at the right rear corner of the main board. Note that the connector coming from the power supply is a female end, and that the plug is keyed to fit on the main board connector only one way. Pin 1 is closest to the front of the computer. Next to this is the key, which is a gap between pins 1 and 2. (You *could* call this a pin, but since nothing is there it is more correctly called, simply, the key.) Even so, make a sketch to help you identify the pins on the main board (a male connector) so that you will plug the two together correctly.

You can do the test quickly without removing the connector by carefully probing the solder points for this connector on the bottom of the board. The power is flowing while you make the measurement, so be very careful.

Due to the design of this particular power supply, it requires an external minimum load. It cannot, and should not, be tested while totally disconnected.

Touch the common probe (black) to pin 6 or pin 8 of the bottom of the connector from the power supply. (Either is a ground, and both are strapped

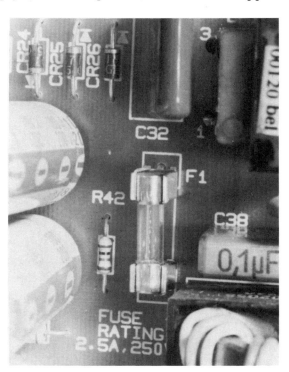

FIG. 5–5 Don't forget to check the fuses.

TABLE 5–1. Power Supply Pin Allocations

Pin	Value	Pin	Value
1	Composite video	6	Ground
key		7	−12 volts DC
2	Horizontal synch	8	Ground
3	Speaker	9	+12 volts DC
4	Vertical synch	10	Battery
5	+5 volts DC		

Note: Some sources list this as an 11-pin connector, with pin 2 being the key. Since there is no physical pin in this spot, I call it a 10-pin connector.

together. You can also attach the black probe to any suitable chassis ground.) Touch the red probe to pin 5. If you get a reading of 4.75 to 5.25 volts, the power supply is working in the 5-volt range. This is the output that allows the circuits to operate, and it is the more critical side. The power supply could be bad if the reading you get is outside this range (see Chapter 6).

If you get an acceptable reading, check the voltage across the 12-volt

FIG. 5–6 Location of power connector to main board.

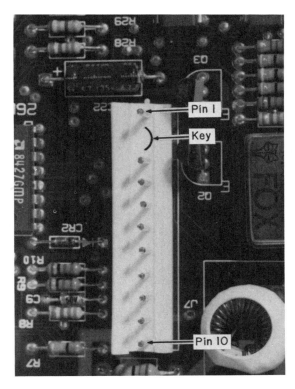

FIG. 5–7 Pin locations on power connector.

side as in the table. With the black probe still touching pin 6 or 8, touch the red probe to pin 9.

Next check pin 7 for −12 volts DC. If you have a digital VOM, the "−" will usually register automatically. Otherwise, reverse the probes (or flip the "Reverse" switch on the VOM), so that the black probe is touching pin 7 and the red probe is touching the ground.

The reading you get should be between 11.25 volts to 12.75 volts. If the readings for both the 5-volt and 12-volt outputs are correct, the power supply is providing the correct voltages. This means that the system board is at fault. If the readings *don't* match, the power supply is probably at fault. Go to the Chapter 6 section on "Power Supply" and run that series of tests.

SPOTTING A FAULTY BOARD

If all readings are correct but the computer will still not power up, there are two possibilities. The power supply could be wearing out and is incapable of producing the needed amount of current. Or else one of the other boards or devices (including the main board) could be faulty and pulling too much current for the power supply to keep up. This doesn't happen often even with computers that have been in use for a long time.

FIG. 5—8 Connector solder points on the bottom of the board.

In the case of a worn power supply, about all you can do it to get a new power supply. Fortunately, this is rarely needed. The next tests help to determine this, and they will also help you spot a malfunctioning board if *that* is the problem. (Before you pull out the old power supply, go to Chapter 6 and continue testing with the information under "The Power Supply.")

There are three parts to this test. The first, and easiest, part will tell you if you have to do the other two parts. For now, go through all three, and jot down the results in Table 5-2 or in the duplicate table in the back of this book. It is critical that you do this while everything is functioning correctly. The readings you get aren't all that important. It's the comparison of the readings while the system is working and those when it fails that counts.

Shut down the power, disconnect all external devices (including the keyboard) and battery, remove the case, and turn the computer onto its side. You'll be probing the solder points of the power connector to the main digital board. Find this strip of pins and identify them.

Set your meter to read resistance. Your goal is to get a listing of the approximate ohms across the various sections of the board. To do this, you'll have to create your own list of readings. This will vary, depending on the VOM you are using and the range in which you set the meter. It's important that you jot down in the table both the range and the brand and model you've used for this test. Again, this has to be done when you know that the digital board is operating perfectly.

Touch the black probe to a known chassis ground. Then touch the red probe to each of the other pins in turn. (Note: You should get zero ohms, or close to it, between pins 6 and 8 and the chassis ground.) You may have to wait a few seconds for the meter to stabilize.

Reach inside and disconnect the internal disk drive, then repeat the probing and jot down the readings you get.

Finally, disconnect the power supply connector from the main digital board and once again take the readings.

Again, this MUST be done when everything is working normally for the measurements to be valid. You will be looking for large changes later, should something be malfunctioning. For example, if you get a 100-ohm reading across two of the pins when everything is working correctly, and get 300,000 ohms when something is malfunctioning, you have probably found the source of the problem. A change of double the first reading generally means nothing other than normal aging of the components. Even a change of ten times your original reading may, or may not, indicate a problem. You are looking for *large* changes.

If something is malfunctioning and you suspect one of the two boards, begin with the first step again. If the readings are close to what you got when everything was functioning, the problem is either something very simple (a burned out fuse, a loose connector, etc.) or is beyond the abilities of anyone without the proper test equipment.

If the readings are greatly different, go to Part Two of the test and remove the internal disk drive connector. If the readings are now within the normal range, you've found the trouble. (It's the drive, in this case.)

If the readings are still out of the normal range, disconnect the power supply connector and probe again. If the readings are normal, the analog (power supply/video) board is the culprit, If they're still way off, the main digital board is at fault.

Two sample readings are provided in Table 5-2. Sample 1 was taken with a Fluke Model D802 set first in the 200-ohm range and then the 2000-ohm range. Sample 2 was taken with a Radio Shack Micronta Model 22-202B set in the 10-ohm and then 1000-ohm range. These readings are merely examples and should not be used as a reliable gauge for your own system. The

TABLE 5–2. Main Board Resistance Check

Meter used (yours) _____

Range used (yours) _____

Pin	Your Reading	Sample 1 (200-ohm range)	Sample 1 (2000-ohm range)	Sample 2 (10-ohm range)	Sample 2 (1000-ohm range)
		Part One—Entire System			
1	_____	over	over	190	10K
2	_____	over	over	200	10K
3	_____	63.4	.063	70	0
4	_____	over	over	160	10K
5	_____	53.0	.051	40	0
6	_____	00.1	.000	0	0
7	_____	over	.761	2000	22K
8	_____	00.1	.000	0	0
9	_____	37.5	.037	35	0
10	_____	over	over	150	9K
		Part Two—Drive Disconnected			
1	_____	over	over	190	10K
2	_____	over	.063	70	0

3	63.6	.063	70	0
4	over	over	160	10K
5	111.0	.097	40	0
6	00.1	.000	0	0
7	over	.759	1800	22K
8	00.1	.000	0	0
9	40.2	.040	35	0
10	over	over	150	9K

Part Three—Main Digital Board Alone

1	over	over	300	10K
2	over	over	500	10K
3	over	over	over	80K
4	over	over	180	10K
5	110.9	.097	110	0
6	00.1	.000	0	0
7	over	.865	10K	28K
8	00.1	.000	0	0
9	over	over	270	14K
10	over	over	150	10K

only way you can trust the readings is to make them with your own meter, and while everything is working.

Before something goes wrong, open your computer and make the measurements. Write the results in this table, or in the duplicate table (Table T-5) in the back of the book.

What seems to be a problem with the main board could be caused by something connected to it. You've taken the first steps toward eliminating these other things earlier in this chapter by observing the symptoms. Unless you have a board to swap with the suspected board, you can generally check only external devices (printers, etc.) and internal devices for power. This is done by disconnecting all possible attached devices and connecting them again one at a time until the system fails (assuming it works at all at any point).

Obviously, you won't be able to disconnect something that is required for system operation. You can't disconnect the main digital board, for example, and expect anything to happen (other than to risk ruining the power supply).

Some external devices draw power from the power supply. Follow the procedure from Chapter 6 on unloading the power supply and then reconnecting the devices one at a time (with the power off each time) to find the one at fault. If the power supply will still not run the computer with all peripheral devices removed, you'll know that the problem is either with the main board or with the power supply. Go to Chapter 6 and thoroughly test the power supply.

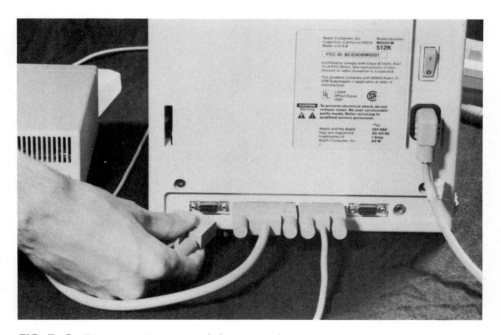

FIG. 5—9 Disconnecting external devices and connectors.

If the main board fails any of these tests, chances are you will have to replace the main board. Unless you have a diagnostics diskette (there are some around), you can't test the various sections. If you happen to have extra chips around the house that match those of the computer, you can try swapping them. Other than that, there isn't much you can do.

CHECK THE OBVIOUS AGAIN

Before you go to a lot of trouble or expense, make sure that you've eliminated all other possible causes of trouble by looking for the obvious once more. Open the cabinet and visually inspect the inside. Is there anything that could be causing an accidental short (like a screw that has fallen onto the board)? Are all boards plugged firmly into place? Are all the cables and connectors secure? (For both things, unplug and reinsert, clean the contacts *with the power off.*)

Outside the cabinet, are the plugs and cables secure? Are they in the right places?

REMOVING THE MAIN BOARD

If tests indicate that the entire main board has to be replaced (rare!), you may wish to do the work yourself. It's not difficult.

To remove the main board, unplug the computer, take off the case, and disconnect everything going to the main board. Be sure to make detailed

FIG. 5–10 Removing the five screws from the case.

sketches so you'll know exactly how everything goes back together. Label everything. It's almost impossible to connect anything incorrectly, but the sketches and labels will make the job easier for you.

The case is held in place by five screws, three of which are hidden: two beneath the handle and one inside the battery case. The case then has to be separated with a case popper or its equivalent. There are two cables attached to the main board. Both must be disconnected before you can slide the board free of the chassis. If it doesn't move easily, you've missed something. *Don't force it!*

Installation is just the reverse. If you've made sketches and have labelled all cables and connectors, you'll have no problems.

OTHER BOARDS

The Macintosh, as it comes from the factory, has only two circuit boards in it. One is the main digital board discussed above. The other, a combined power supply and video board, is covered in Chapters 4 and 6.

However, most peripherals have at least one circuit board down inside. Without sophisticated test equipment, you probably won't find a specific problem with a circuit board. Generally, the fastest, easiest way to test a particular board is to swap it with one you know to be good. If everything works again, you'll have found the problem.

You can do a few simple things on your own, mostly through a process of elimination.

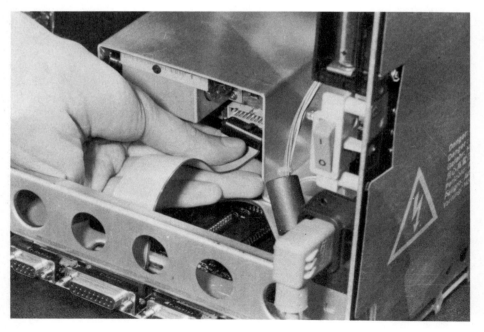

FIG. 5–11 Remove the drive and power supply connectors from the main board.

FIG. 5—12 The board will now slide out easily.

The obvious first step is to track the problem to the particular device. When testing the main board as detailed above, you may have found that a certain connected device is dragging down the entire computer. If the computer has been operating correctly except for one function, you can usually eliminate the functioning devices.

For example, if the printer is malfunctioning but the computer is running fine otherwise, it isn't necessarily the printer that is at fault, but it's highly unlikely that the disk drive or monitor is causing the problem. It could be the computer, the program, the cable, or the printer. Your first job is to find out which of these it is.

If one program runs the printer perfectly and another does not, the fault is with the program (or an incompatibility between program and printer). The cable can be eliminated by testing it for continuity. (Set your VOM to read resistance and check each wire in the cable. Zero ohms means the wire is good; infinite ohms means that the cable is at fault.)

That leaves the computer or the printer. The easiest way to find out is to connect another printer that is compatible with the Macintosh. Assuming that the printer has a built-in self test, run this. If it doesn't work, you've found the problem. (If it *does* work, the printer is probably not at fault, but could be. In particular, the connector in the printer could be faulty. The self-test will run just fine, but the bad connector could be preventing data from reaching the printer.)

Now visually check the suspected device. Don't forget the obvious things, such as power cords and fuses. Are all cables going to it tight and clean? Have any of the components inside worked loose? (Don't forget to shut down the power before removing or inserting any board, cable, or device, and before pushing on the components to make sure that they are seated properly.)

If the device has a plug-in board, try cleaning the contacts with a high-quality electronic cleaner (*not* a television tuner cleaner, which will leave a residue!). If you don't have a cleaner around, you can use a soft pencil eraser for flat connectors, making sure that you don't get any particles inside the computer. For pin-type connectors, spend the time and money to get a high-quality cleaner. Any other method is fairly certain to cause more harm than good.

It's helpful, if not essential, to know the function of a particular circuit board. Once you know this, testing can go smoothly. A power supply board can be tested for input and output, regardless of whether the board is the power supply of the Macintosh or of a printer (see Chapter 6). Other boards should be tested for power in (and power out, depending on the circumstances).

Carefully probe with your VOM set to resistance and then DC voltage, set to 30+ volts to be safe (when you're uncertain of a voltage level, *always* start high and work down). This testing can reveal quite a few specifics about the inputs and outputs of a particular board. A digital logic probe or oscilloscope (both beyond the scope of this book) will help to spot which pins do what.

If the suspected board or device is new to your system, you must ask yourself "Has it ever worked?" Have you made any other changes to the system?

SUMMARY

Diagnosis of circuit board problems is often difficult and time-consuming. Even professional repair shops commonly track the problem to a particular board and then just replace that board. By observation and note taking, you should be able to isolate the malfunctioning board quickly.

As always, take some time to visually inspect for the obvious. Are all cables and wires firmly attached? Are they connected correctly? If the suspected board is not the original or an exact replacement, is it compatible and designed to work with your Macintosh? Has it changed something else?

Fortunately, if a board operates when you first install it, it will probably continue to function for many years. No maintenance is required.

Chapter 6
Power Supplies, Keyboards, Printers, and Monitors

You can connect a number of different devices to your Macintosh. Since there are so many different options, so many different manufacturers, and so many variables, it is impossible to cover them all. Only the most common options are included in this chapter. These should give you some basic guidelines for repair.

Use the information in Chapter 2 before you begin poking around in the machinery. The steps taken in Chapter 2 should have directed you to this chapter.

POWER SUPPLY DIAGNOSTICS

The driving force behind the Macintosh is the power supply. It does just what the name implies. It takes the 120 volts at 60 cycles per second from the wall outlet and changes it to a clean, steady 5- and 12-volt DC supply for the computer circuits.

Normally it does its job just fine and gives no problems. Unlike the power supplies of some other computers, the Macintosh power supply is relatively tough. Chances are you'll never have to worry about anything going wrong with the supply other than the mechanical on-off switch in the back.

If the power supply *is* acting up, you may not be readily able to spot it as the source of the problem. The computer might seem to be completely dead. This could be caused by the power supply, but it could also be a problem with the system board or from a combination of other things. Your computer could also seem to be operating normally except for a data read/write problem. You might be inclined to automatically place the blame on the memory

FIG. 6—1 The power supply and video circuits make up the analog board.

or on the drives, while the actual cause *could* be with the power supply. Don't replace anything until you know for sure.

General diagnosis is the same for all power supplies. Is power getting to it? Is it kicking out the correct voltage values and with sufficient current? The details below concentrate on the power supply of the Macintosh itself. However, the same basic steps can be used for virtually any power supply, such as those in your peripherals.

The power supply in the Macintosh is of the switching type. This means that power is provided by the digital components switching on and off quickly. This is an extremely efficient means for operation. It also allows the power supply to be smaller and to run cooler. However, repairs on such a power supply are extremely difficult. "Repair" is normally by replacement of the power supply unit.

If nothing happens when you flip the power switch, you are likely to accuse the power supply without further thinking. This symptom could mean that the power supply has died. It could also mean that something else is wrong.

If the problem is outside the power supply, the power supply will try to reset itself. Each time this cycle occurs, the oscillator passes through an audible range and produces a soft click that you may be able to hear. If you hear this steady click, click, click, the power supply is working (or is trying to). Finding out for sure isn't difficult.

INCOMING POWER

If power is obviously present (i.e., the cooling fan is running, or you hear the clicking) you can skip this first check. If nothing at all is happening, begin with this step.

The first things to check are the fuses, the power cord, the plug, the outlets, and the power switches. Once you have done this and know that power is getting to the power supply, you have eliminated the obvious. You've also started the process of isolating the problem.

As mentioned in Chapter 2, you can use a lamp or any number of other things to check the outlet for power, but it is better to check it with a meter. The power supply operates in the range of 100 volts and 130 volts. A lamp will operate beyond these ranges without any apparent difference, but the power supply of the computer will either begin to operate erratically or may even shut itself down. Until you've checked the outlet with a meter, you won't know for certain if the problem is in the computer or in the lines that supply the outlet. (More information on using a meter to check outlets is contained in Chapters 1 and 2.)

If the outlet is good, check the fuse to the power supply. For the Macintosh, this fuse is inside the computer on the analog board. Other devices, such as the ImageWriter, have an external fuse, which makes checking it easier. If the fuse is good, the problem is somewhere between the power

FIG. 6-2 Checking the fuse can be done visually. Better yet, use your VOM and test for continuity.

FIG. 6—3 Checking an outlet with a meter.

supply and the wall outlet. One by one, eliminate the fuse, switch, and power cord. If you do get the correct reading (and the power supply fuse is good), go to the next step and check the power supply output.

POWER SUPPLY OUTPUT

If power is getting to the power supply, but nothing is happening, it's time to see if the power supply is putting out the correct voltages. It is designed to supply both 5 volts and 12 volts DC.

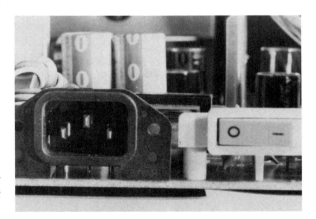

FIG. 6—4 Be extremely careful when checking for AC power.

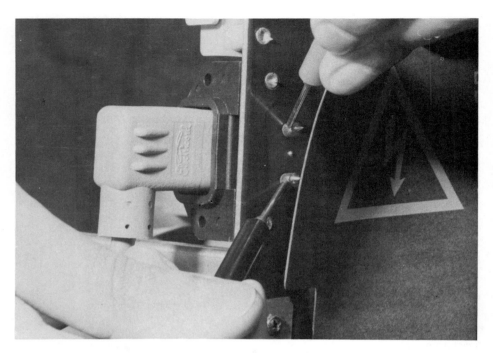

FIG. 6—5 Checking the voltage to the power supply.

There are two ways to check this. The first and easiest part involves checking the power output to the external connectors. (This test is also the least conclusive.) The second part is more thorough and involves directly testing the power output by probing the pins where the power supply provides power to the main digital board.

Essentially, the power flow begins at the wall outlet and goes into the power supply. Here it is changed into the needed voltages for the computer. A part of it goes to the video circuits. One multi-pinned cable goes from the power supply to the main digital board. From here it goes to various other devices, both internal and external.

Some of the external devices used in a complete Macintosh system take power from the power supply indirectly through the main board. The external disk drive is a good example. It draws power from the power supply through the main digital board. Most external devices that take current from the computer's power supply do it in this way.

The following standard devices will take power from the computer's power supply: internally—the video circuits, the main digital board, and the disk drive; externally—the keyboard, the mouse, some modems, and the external floppy disk drive.

One thing to be careful of is when something non-standard has been added to the computer. If you've made that modification yourself, you will know where it taps into the power. If someone else has made that unusual

Front View

4 3 2 1

Keyboard Connector

1. Ground
2. Keyboard Clock
3. Keyboard Data
4. +5VDC

Cable colors
1. Black
2. Red
3. Green
4. Yellow

FIG. 6—6 Keyboard pin allocations.

modification, it may take some looking and probing to find out where the modification taps in for power.

If everything is completely dead, it could be that something external is dragging down the computer. Shut off the power and disconnect everything external. Then, with the power off between each connection, reconnect each device, one at a time until the system fails again.

Now try a different order of reconnection, starting with the device that caused the failure the first time. (If the first reconnection caused a failure, start with another device.)

You can also measure the output directly at the connector with your VOM. Shut off the power and disconnect at the computer the powered de-

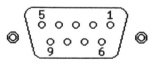

Mouse Connector

1. Ground
2. +5VDC
3. Ground
4. X2 pulses
5. X1 pulses
6. NC
7. SWITCH
8. Y2 pulses
9. Y1 pulses

FIG. 6—7 Mouse pin allocations.

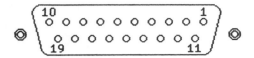

External Disk Connector

1. Ground	11. Phase 0
2. Ground	12. Phase 1
3. Ground	13. Phase 2
4. Ground	14. Phase 3
5. -12VDC	15. Write Req
6. +5VDC	16. Head Select
7. +12VDC	17. Enable
8. +12VDC	18. Read
9. NC	19. Write
10. PWM (motor)	

FIG. 6—8 External drive pin allocations.

vice to be tested. Once it is disconnected, you can flip the power back on again. With the VOM set to read 12 volts, touch the black probe to the ground pin of the connector you are testing. Then touch the red probe to those pins that are supposed to be supplying voltage to the device.

It's possible to get inconsistent or incorrect results from this test. If the power supply is just starting to go, it may test correctly but may not be able to produce sufficient current to drive everything. In this case, the previous test should also give inconsistent results.

It should be obvious that units with their own separate power supplies will not take power from the computer's supply. A hard drive, for example,

FIG. 6—9 Location of power supply connector on the main digital board.

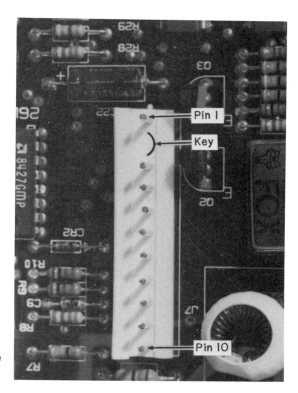

FIG. 6—10 Close up of the main board power connector.

will almost always have its own supply. It's highly unlikely that these units will be dragging down the power supply of the Macintosh.

If a device is suspect, go to the appropriate section in this book for further help (e.g., if the offending device is the disk drive, go to Chapter 4). If the power supply seems to be at fault, continue to the next test.

This test checks power to the main board. It involves the use of your multimeter set to the 12-volt DC range. The test points are where the cable from the power supply plugs into the system board (see Fig. 6—9 through 6—14 and Table 6—1). The power is on during these tests. You must be extremely careful to not cause any short circuits.

TABLE 6—1. Power Supply Pin Allocations

Pin	Use	Pin	Use
1	Composite video	6	Ground
key	(no pin)	7	−12 volts DC
2	Horizontal synch	8	Ground
3	Speaker	9	+12 volts DC
4	Vertical synch	10	Battery
5	+5 volts DC		

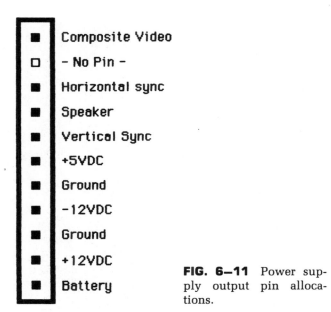

- Composite Video
- – No Pin –
- Horizontal sync
- Speaker
- Vertical Sync
- +5VDC
- Ground
- –12VDC
- Ground
- +12VDC
- Battery

FIG. 6—11 Power supply output pin allocations.

Toward the front of the power supply and under the CRT is the 10-pin output connector that supplies power to everything else. This strip is keyed, with a gap between pins 1 and 2. The cable itself has this spot filled in, thus making it impossible to connect things backwards. It's important that you first identify the correct pin numbers, especially since the actual probing takes place under the circuit board. If you get them backwards (i.e., thinking that pin 1 is pin 10) you could end up in trouble. You'll use pin 9 to test for 12 volts DC. If you make a mistake and touch the probe to pin 1, you're actually touching a pin carrying the video signal.

The video circuitry is a part of the analog board. The power supply feeds them directly. There are two cables for this, both of which carry high voltage and shouldn't be touched unless you know exactly what you're doing and have experience with high voltage circuits.

This test is easier, and safer, to perform if you probe the power supply connector from the bottom of the main digital board. This way you have easier access to the output pins without coming near the dangerous voltage points around the CRT. It also allows you to check the power supply itself while it has the proper load on it. If a device connected to the power supply is faulty, it could be dragging the power supply down. For even greater safety, hook the black (ground) probe to a known chassis ground, and use only the red probe. This allows you to concentrate on just the one probe.

Pins 6 and 8 are common (ground). The black probe of the meter goes to either of these two, or to a known chassis ground as just mentioned. Set the meter to read 12 volts DC. (Keep in mind that the power is ON during these tests! PROCEED CAREFULLY!) Touch the red probe to pin 5. The reading

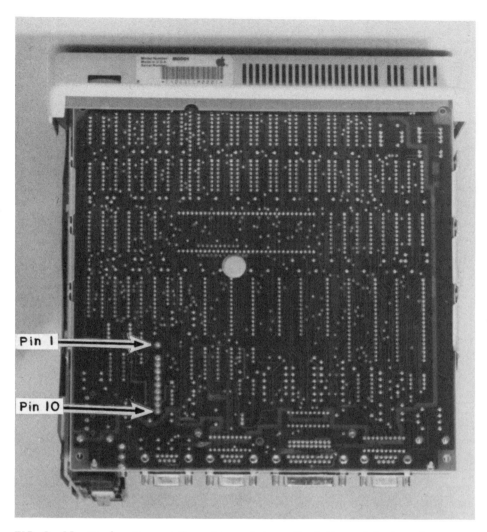

FIG. 6–12 Pin locations at the solder points on the bottom of the board.

should be 5 volts. Touching the red probe to pin 9 should give a 12-volt reading. If either of these is incorrect, the power supply may be failing, and certainly has a problem getting power to the main digital board.

Pin 1 of this connector is closest to the front of the computer, and away from the ports. The space between pins 1 and 2 is keyed to prevent attaching the connector incorrectly. In this case, the connector on the board is missing a pin, and the cable has this slot filled in.

It's unlikely that the power cable is bad, but you can quickly find out by testing continuity across the cable. The way to find out is to disconnect the cable from the power supply and the main board (*with the power off!*) and probe the cable for continuity. Each set of pins should show zero ohms across the cable.

FIG. 6—13 Probing the solder points on the bottom of the board.

FIG. 6—14 The 10-pin power supply connector is the white plug near the center of the photograph.

FIG. 6–15 The power connector is close to the CRT. Be very careful to stay away from the CRT. The correct place to probe is on the bottom of the main digital board at the connector solder points.

This also gives you the chance to visually inspect the pins. Look for any discoloration. Sometimes these pins overheat, which causes a poor connection and partially or completely blocks the flow of power.

Remember to shut off the power before disconnecting and again before reconnecting!

If these voltages aren't correct, you can guess that the problem is in the power supply or in the cable. The continuity check of the cable eliminates

FIG. 6–16 Be extremely careful when near the power supply board. This connector carries high voltage for the CRT. *Don't touch!*

FIG. 6—17 This connector also carries a high voltage for the CRT. Again, *don't touch*.

this possibility. If the power supply is bad, all you can do is replace the faulty unit (with an exact match). If the voltage readings are correct proceed to the next step.

DISK DRIVE POWER

This step tests if power is getting to the drives. It can be skipped if the drives seem to be operating correctly. If the drives have been causing trouble, you

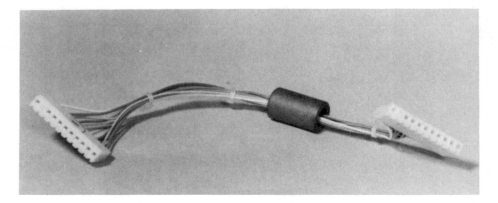

FIG. 6—18 The power supply cable for the main board.

FIG. 6—19 Location of drive cable.

can find out quickly if the problem is in the drives, in the power supply, or in the drive cable.

Power to the drives comes from the power supply, through the main board, and along the connecting cable. The internal drive uses a flat ribbon-cable. The external drive uses a round cable with 19 pins on the computer side, and 20 pins on the connector inside the external drive itself. You can test for power either with the cable still attached, or with the cable un-

FIG. 6—20 An easy, and excellent, way to probe is at the solder joints on the board.

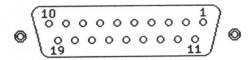

External Disk Connector

1. Ground	11. Phase 0
2. Ground	12. Phase 1
3. Ground	13. Phase 2
4. Ground	14. Phase 3
5. –12VDC	15. Write Req
6. +5VDC	16. Head Select
7. +12VDC	17. Enable
8. +12VDC	18. Read
9. NC	19. Write
10. PWM (motor)	

FIG. 6–21 External disk drive power pin allocations.

plugged. If you suspect that the drive is causing the problem, it is best to unplug the cable and test from this cable or at the connector on the computer.

REPLACING THE POWER SUPPLY

The power supply is tucked inside the computer and along the side. Since there are only two boards in the Mac, it's easy to find. Since the same board also provides and carries the high voltage for the CRT, it is best to let the computer sit unplugged for at least six hours before you begin. This will allow the dangerous voltage to bleed off. Even then, proceed carefully.

FIG. 6–22 Remove the holding screws from the back of the chassis, then carefully remove the case.

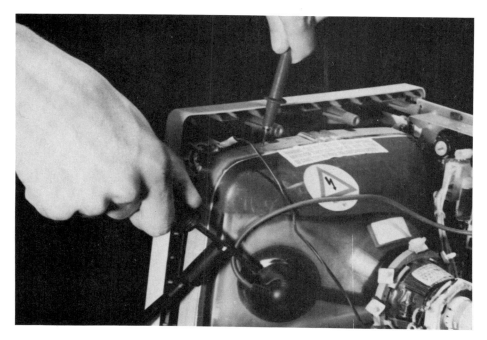

FIG. 6–23 Even if you've let the computer sit for a while to drain off the high voltage, short it yourself just to be sure—and safe!

FIG. 6–24 Carefully label and disconnect everything going to and from the power supply.

Chilton's Guide to Macintosh Repair and Maintenance
POWER SUPPLIES, KEYBOARDS, PRINTERS, AND MONITORS

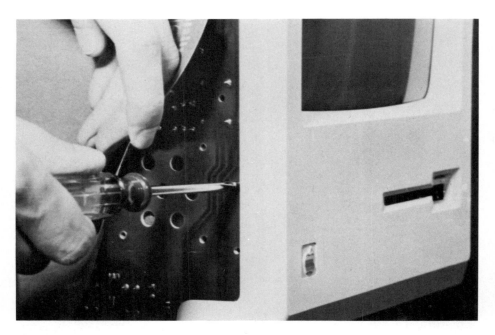

FIG. 6—25 Remove the three holding screws.

The power supply is held in place by three screws. Two are located near the power switch. The third is toward the front of the board. After you've labelled and disconnected all wires going to the power supply, remove these screws. The power supply will lift out easily. Installation of the new power supply is just the reverse of this.

THE KEYBOARD

Each key on the keyboard is a switch. As you press down on the key, contact is made and the appropriate signal is sent to the computer by the circuitry. The keyboard does pre-processing for the character generation, using an Intel 8021 IC.

Some of the IC chips on the keyboard are extremely sensitive to static electricity. They can be damaged if you even touch them with your fingers. If you *must* touch them, be sure that you have drained off any static charge in your body, such as by placing your other hand on the case of the power supply or by touching some other reliable ground.

Although the keys and keyboard are durable, like anything else, they can cause trouble or quit working entirely. When this happens, the easiest and quickest solution is to replace the entire keyboard. But before you toss out the malfunctioning keyboard, run a few simple tests. The problem might actually be elsewhere, or could be something that is easily fixed.

As always, begin with the obvious. Is the keyboard plugged in? Is it plugged in correctly? The keyboard plug looks like a modular telephone

FIG. 6—26 The power supply will now lift out easily.

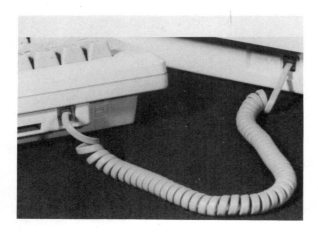

FIG. 6–27 If the keyboard seems to be malfunctioning, a good place to start your diagnosis is to check the plug.

plug. In actuality, it's quite different. If someone tried to connect the computer to the telephone line through this port (it has happened), damage could have been done to the computer. The same is true if someone hooked the keyboard directly to the phone line.

The keyboard cable uses wires with a lower resistance than standard telephone cable. If you're using an extension cable for the keyboard, it must have wires of the same resistance value. A cable made from telephone wire probably won't work reliably, if at all.

FIG. 6–28 Closeup of the keyboard connector on the main board.

Front View

Keyboard Connector

1. Ground
2. Keyboard Clock
3. Keyboard Data
4. +5VDC

Cable colors

1. Black

2. Red

FIG. 6–29 Keyboard   **3. Green**

pin allocations.   **4. Yellow**

If the keyboard is doing nothing, but is attached correctly, it might not be getting power. Set your meter to read 5 volts. Touch the black probe to pin 1, and the red probe to pin 4. It's best to do this first at the computer, either with the keyboard plugged in or with it unplugged and probing directly at the connector. You can also probe at the keyboard end of the cable, preferably at the cable connector after it has been unplugged, and again inside the keyboard at the solder joints of this connector.

With the power off and the keyboard cable disconnected from both ends, set your meter to read resistance (ohms) and test the continuity in the cable. You can find out quickly if the problem is in the cable. This is done by touching the meter probes to the ends of each of the wires in the keyboard cable. The reading should be almost 0 ohms between the ends of each of the four wires. If there is a break in the wire, the reading will be infinity. In this case, replace the cable, and you're back in business.

Do not replace the cable with a standard telephone cable. The two look very much alike, but are not the same electrically. A telephone cable, properly wired, *may* work, but can give intermittent operating problems. The shorter the cable, the better, if you use telephone wire. And if you must, be sure that all four pins are connected (with some telephone plugs, only two or three are connected), and that the cable uses "real wire" instead of the spun copper sometimes found in telephone cable.

The keyboard is held together by five screws on the bottom of the keyboard assembly. With these screws removed, the keyboard comes apart easily.

With the cover off, you'll see where the cable connector attaches to the keyboard circuit. Refer to Fig. 6–29 and Table 6–2 for the pin-out. Pin 1

TABLE 6—2.
Keyboard Pins

Pin	Wire Color	Use
1	Black	Ground
2	Red	Keyboard clock
3	Green	Keyboard data
4	Yellow	+5 volts DC

(with the black wire) is ground. Pin 4 (yellow wire) is the 5 volt DC input. By touching the probes of your meter across these two pins (CAREFULLY! Don't cause a short!!!) you can find out if power is getting to the keyboard. This can be tested at the computer, at the keyboard side of the cable, or at the keyboard connector. If voltage is present, and if the keyboard is still dead, the keyboard circuitry is faulty.

Inside the keyboard are the electronics. Those electronics handle the signals between the keyboard and the computer. Unlike the keys themselves, the electronics are prone to damage from fluid. To protect your keyboard, keep *all* fluids away from the board.

You've probably heard some of the horror stories about liquid falling into a computer keyboard. One of the strangest I've ever heard involves a man who decided that a cute photo would be one of his two-month old baby sitting on the keyboard in front of the computer. The child has an "accident." Obviously so did the keyboard. The acidic fluid (let's keep it clean, now) caused bad connections on the soldered components and even damaged the circuit board. This made a simple repair impossible. The whole keyboard had to be replaced.

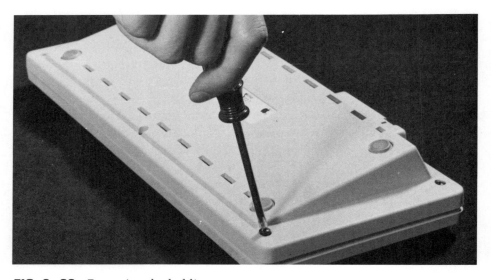

FIG. 6—30 Removing the holding screws.

FIG. 6–31 With the cover removed, it's easy to check the pins on the logic board.

In a sense, you test the keys each time you use the keyboard. To test an individual key electronically, you'll have to remove the keyboard case and the assembly. Set your meter to read resistance (ohms). On the bottom of the assembly you'll see a number of traces (parts of the circuit board that act as wires). Trying to locate which points are which isn't easy, but if you're patient you should be able to find the appropriate points. Touch the probes, one to each of the traces of that particular key. The reading should be infinite, showing that there is no pathway. When you press the key, the resistance should drop to almost zero. If this doesn't happen, the keyswitch needs to be replaced.

FIG. 6–32 The disassembled keyboard.

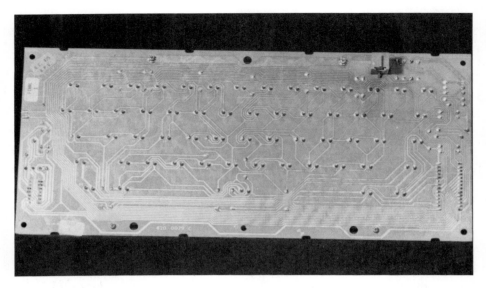

FIG. 6–33 The bottom of the circuit board. To replace a keyswitch, your first job will be to locate the two traces to that particular key.

CHANGING A KEYSWITCH

Changing a key isn't an easy job. To do it you will need a high-quality soldering tool and some experience in using it. If the heated tip touches the circuit board for more than about 3 seconds, the heat could lift the tracing from the board. Melt the solder on the pins of the switch. A desoldering tool is very helpful in removing the melted solder. If you've done everything right, the key should come out easily. *Don't* force it.

The new key is installed in reverse order. Once again, be very careful when using the soldering tool. If you don't have experience with soldering, leave the job to a professional. Soldering is not as easy as it seems. In fact, most people prefer to replace the whole assembly, rather than going through the time and bother.

Even if you want to attempt a keyswitch replacement, finding the replacement part is going to be tough.

THE MOUSE

Macintosh advertising says "If you can point, you can operate the Macintosh." This is done with the mouse, which you run like a pointer around on the screen and then push a button to carry out the needed command.

As powerful as is this feature, there is actually very little to go wrong with the mouse. The most common cause of malfunction is dirt getting in

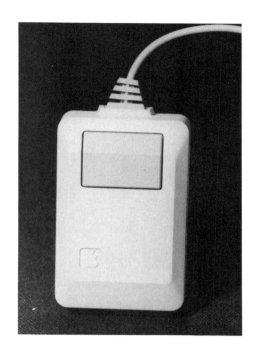

FIG. 6—34 The mouse.

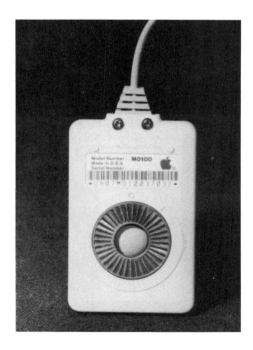

FIG. 6—35 The bottom of the mouse, showing the rolling ball.

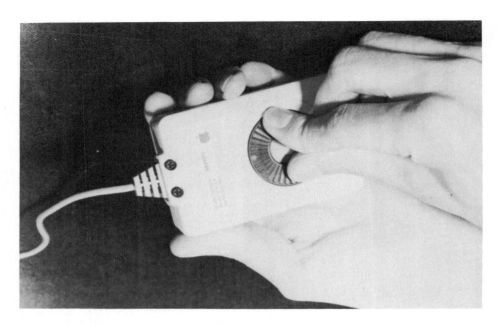

FIG. 6—36 To clean the ball, turn the mouse over and turn the holding ring.

and around the roller. The solution is a regular cleaning of the ball and chamber.

For cleaning the ball, use a dry, clean cloth. Be careful not to get any lint or other contamination on the ball. Never use any cleaning fluid on this ball.

The inside of the chamber is a natural collecting point for dust. Begin by blowing out the chamber, preferably with a can of moisture-free compressed air, such as can be found in many photographic supply stores.

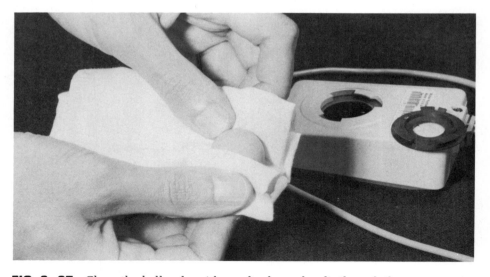

FIG. 6—37 Clean the ball only with a soft, clean, dry, lintless cloth.

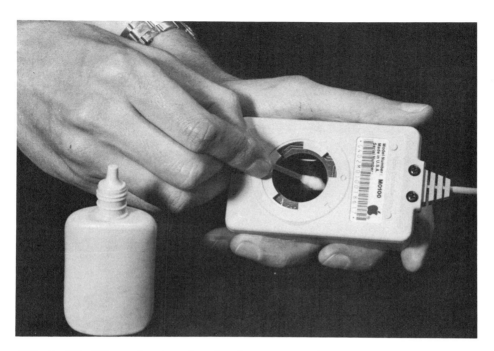

FIG. 6—38 When cleaning the chamber, use a tight swab and a high quality cleaner.

FIG. 6—39 With the mouse completely disassembled, you can more easily get to the roller for cleaning. Tweezers can help to remove hairs, etc. from the works.

There are two rollers inside the chamber. These can be cleaned with a cotton swab. Be sure that the swab has a tight tip on it. Any high-quality cleaning fluid may be used, such as tape head cleaner or pure isopropyl alcohol. *Do not* use alcohol off the shelf. This is only about 70% alcohol (if that much), with the other 30% being water, oils, and other materials. Use *only* technical grade isopropyl alcohol, of at least 90%. (I take the time to find the 99% grade.)

PRINTERS

There are many different printers available. Each has its own characteristics and construction. One might require a partial disassembly to just reset the switches. Another will have a built-in memory buffer. Still another could have the dual capabilities of both computer printer and standard typewriter. There are differences in speed, print quality, and printing technologies. The printer may require a serial connection, a parallel connection, or may allow you to choose which you prefer. Some may even require some special software patched to your regular programs.

The design of the Macintosh makes many printers unusable, or usable only after some complicated and often expensive modifications.

The manual that came with your printer is the best source for specific information on printer operation and maintenance. Become familiar with both the printer and the manual. Find out what capabilities your printer has (and doesn't have) and how to take care of various problems that could come up.

PRINTER CONNECTIONS

Many printers give you the option of connecting it either as a parallel device or as a serial device. Parallel is the more common means of connecting a printer for several reasons. If the computer has one port of each type, the serial port is usually kept open for communications, because devices such as modems require a serial connection. By connecting the printer as a parallel device, the serial port is kept available. With the Macintosh, this is meaningless since there are no parallel ports. The only time this will matter to you is if you install one of the several devices on the market that convert the serial I/O of the Macintosh to parallel.

Since the printer is a mechanical device, it is prone to more wear and tear than most things connected to the computer. It has at least two motors (for head and platen) and may have more. The print head moves back and forth across the platen, and also either spins (as with a daisywheel printer) or has a print head that makes characters by punching at the paper with wires (dot matrix printer). All this motion causes wear. It can also create fair amounts of heat. If allowed to build up, heat can cause all sorts of damage, both mechanical and electronic.

FIG. 6—40 Printer port is on the right. External drive is on the left.

The first thing to do is to get out the manual for your printer and get familiar with the information. Many manuals give specific error signals to let you know what has gone wrong. Also included will be information specific to your printer, such as how to remove the platen and other parts to free up a paper jam, how to load the ribbon, and so forth.

Paper can jam as it feeds through the printer. Even single sheets can cause a paper jam. Printers that use multiple sheets (with sheet loader or tractor) are even more prone to jams. Jams also tend to be more common if your printer is connected as a serial device. When a jam occurs, the printer can grind to a halt. Sometimes the jam isn't apparent. A few printers require a fairly complicated disassembly to get at it. (See Appendix B.)

If the ribbon isn't installed properly, all sorts of strange things can happen. Part of a character might print, leaving the other part weak or nonexistent. It could shut down the printer entirely, or print a couple of characters and then act as though the signal had stopped.

In some printers the end of the ribbon is sensed by a small switch. As the ribbon reaches its end, the switch stops the printer. This switch can also signal that the ribbon is used up if the cartridge isn't attached properly or if

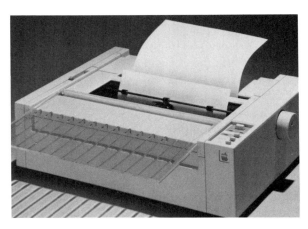

FIG. 6—41 The Apple ImageWriter is a high-speed, serial dot matrix printer.

the switch fails. Other printers feed the ribbon through continuously. When the print gets light, you replace the ribbon.

Many printers have a safety switch in the lid. Lift the lid and the switch tells the printer to stop. It will also tell the printer to stop if the lid isn't closed all the way, or if the switch is faulty.

If the printer is not making an impression, remove the paper and look for indentations. The print head will make indentations in the paper if it is working, even if the ribbon is not. If the paper has the marks from the print head, the ribbon or ribbon advance mechanism is causing the problem.

There are lots of adjustments possible with most printers. There are the usual adjustments for spacing and forms thickness (number of sheets), the release catches, plus others. Just as a typewriter won't function properly if the adjustments aren't correct, neither will the computer's printer. Most of the time a printer problem will be something very simple.

By performing occasional maintenance checks and cleaning the printer, you can greatly reduce the malfunctions. Clean the ribbon guides, print shield, and the inside of the machine. A build-up of ink or paper dust can cause problems. If your printer has a built-in self-test, run it occasionally. (Run it once when you first get the machine and know that the printer is operating correctly. How else will you know what the results of the test are supposed to be?)

Note: To activate the self-test on the ImageWriter, shut off the power, push and hold the Form Feed button, and turn on the power while holding this button. The test will continue until you shut off the power again.

This self-test allows you to carry the diagnostics one step further. If the test shows that the printer is operating correctly, you'll know that the problem is in the printer interface, in the cable, or in the computer. You can eliminate the cable by testing for continuity with your meter. The diagnostics diskette can tell you if the printer port is functioning correctly at the computer. About the only thing left is the interface in the printer itself.

PRINTER DIAGNOSIS

If there seems to be no power going to the printer, check the outlet, the power cord, and the fuse before assuming that the problem lies in the power supply. If power is obviously present you can skip all power checks and go to the more detailed diagnostic steps, such as running the self-test of the printer (if it has one).

If power is getting to the printer but nothing happens, check once again all cables, connectors, switches, and the software itself. You can eliminate some things simply by knowing that the printer once functioned as it should.

The self-test cycle of the printer (if it has one) should give you a good idea of where the problem is. If the self-test operates, the printer itself is likely to be just fine. The problem is then more likely to be inside the computer or in the cable. You can easily eliminate the cable as the possible cause by using your meter.

Disconnect the printer cable. With the meter set to read resistance, touch the black probe to a pin on one end of the cable and the red probe to the same pin on the opposite side. A reading of near zero ohms means that the wire between the pins is good. An infinite reading shows that the wire in the cable is broken, or that those pins are not used.

The cable between the computer and the printer has up to 25 pins. Five pins on the 9-pin connector are standard from the Macintosh itself, and 4 pins are used at the printer; more pins are possible if you are using some kind of interface box. Some pins are not connected to anything and will give a reading as if the wire inside is broken. The printer manual should tell you which pins are used and which are not. Without this, you'll have to take the cable heads apart to know the wiring. (The standard Macintosh cable heads are molded and cannot be taken apart. Refer to the printer port pin allocation chart at the end of this book. The only time you'll be able to take apart the head is when the cable was custom made.) Inside, the wires are probably color-coded. If even one wire is broken inside the cable, or if just one isn't making proper contact with the connector, the printer might refuse to function.

Refer to the printer manual for the correct switch settings. If these aren't set correctly, the best the printer can do is punch out meaningless garbage. It is also important to have the software you are using "installed" (getting that piece of software compatible with your printer), if the program calls for this. (The procedure for this is usually in the software documentation.)

VIDEO PROBLEMS

Monitor problems are usually obvious. The screen may be blank, which could be due to something as simple as having touched the contrast control. It may show an incorrect display. It could have an image that is tilted, too small, too large, out of focus, too dim, and so on. If the image on the screen is out of whack, the problem is probably with the monitor itself. If the problem isn't in the monitor, there are only a few other places it could be. You can find out quickly by running a few tests.

Unfortunately, working with the video circuits of the Macintosh brings along several dangers. Testing and adjusting can be done only with power flowing. And the power you'll be coming into contact with is potentially deadly.

The CRT requires a high voltage to operate. If this isn't dangerous enough to keep you clear of the monitor section, trying to reach those circuits often means that you will have your hand very near the incoming 120 volts. A piece of insulated tape, such as black electrical tape, placed over the fuse and other hot spots can reduce the risk to you. It can't remove it entirely. (Obviously, have the power shut off when putting the tape over the fuse.)

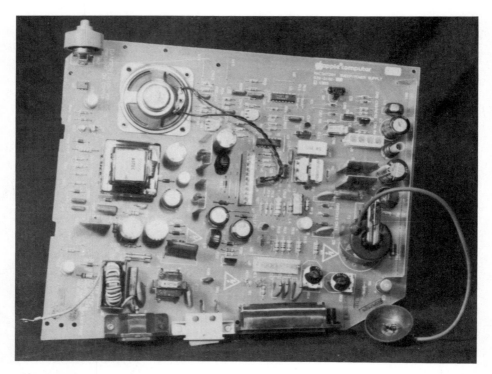

FIG. 6–42 The video board and power supply board are the same unit.

One very simple thing can be done. With the cabinet off (and power on), look at (*don't touch!*) the neck of the video tube. Under a dim light you should be able to see a soft glow. If this glow is present, chances are good that the CRT itself is not at fault. The problem is more likely in this case to be in the video section of the combined-function analog board.

Before going any further, it is advised that you leave any and all video problems to a professional. The money you spend is a worthwhile investment just for your own protection. Even if the circuits involved were safe, adjustments are difficult to make. That alone is a good reason for taking this kind of job to a professional.

One client brought in a malfunctioning computer to the service center. Everything had been working just fine, he said, until his two nephews were playing some games on the machine and suddenly the screen went blank. Nothing he did could get it to work again, and he was pretty sure that they'd damaged something. As it turned out, one of the nephews had apparently touched the brightness control.

Check this knob before you do anything else, even if you're sure that it hasn't been touched.

All other adjustments are made on the video driver section inside the computer. Again, this is a dangerous job, best left to professionals. If you're determined to do it on your own, be extra careful, especially around the

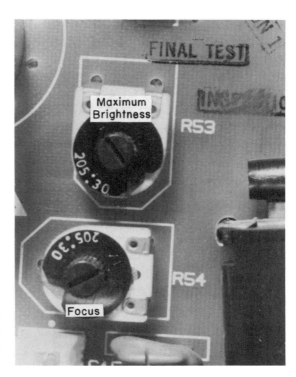

FIG. 6–43 Two of the video controls on the analog board: the brightness and focus. Don't fiddle with either of them.

power supply. To make the adjustments, you'll need a set of alignment tools. Use only the all plastic tools. Even a tiny metal tip will make adjustment impossible. (The professional also has the benefit of a special video alignment diskette—something unavailable to the computer owner. Without this diskette, all you do is to make a guess.)

A sudden change in the display during operation indicates that something besides the manual adjustments is wrong. A simple adjustment probably won't help. If this happens, make detailed notes of what is happening and when. Then take your computer to a professional.

SUMMARY

Power supply problems are not always obvious. The built-in protective circuitry may shut down the power if something is wrong elsewhere in the system. A "nothing happens" situation does not necessarily mean that the power supply is at fault.

Testing the power supply is a matter of eliminating devices one at a time, and of taking a few voltage measurements. Within a few minutes you should be able to isolate the problem.

The keyboard is tested constantly. You test it yourself merely by using it. If pushing a key consistently does nothing, or if the key simply feels wrong, you'll know that it's time to perform a more thorough testing, or that it's time to replace the individual key or the keyboard itself.

Printers are famous for giving troubles. They are mechanical devices with at least two motors spinning along. Just connecting a non-standard printer in the first place can be a frustrating chore. Once it is up and working, keep it that way by some occasional maintenance, such as cleaning out the paper dust.

As with printers, a malfunction of the monitor is generally obvious. Begin by eliminating other possible causes, such as the brightness control knob. If you haven't found the problem after this, it is *far* better to abandon further attempts at repair and take the computer to a professional. There is considerable danger involved in working around the video section of your computer. Even if you don't mind risking your life, proper repair or adjustment requires special tools. Leave it to someone who knows and who has the proper tools and software.

Chapter 7
Periodic Maintenance

The Macintosh is so well designed and constructed that there isn't much to be done as far as maintenance goes. (In fact, the people at Apple built the Macintosh so that it would not require much maintenance.) As with all computers, most of the activity takes place inside the circuits. There is very little to adjust or clean, almost nothing to go wrong.

Even so, you can reduce repair costs and aggravation by performing a few simple maintenance checks now and then.

THE ENVIRONMENT

The most important factor in the overall health of your computer system is its surroundings. The more dust and other contaminants that are around, the more often your system will give you trouble.

One owner used his computer to keep track of his electroplating company. The computer was kept separate from the plant, but not separate enough. The acidic fumes were obvious, both to the nose and to the computer. Every few months he would have a major computer failure. Twice in the first year he had to replace the drives, and once the entire system board.

Another company hired an operator who smoked heavily. Within a few months one of the drives was malfunctioning. When opened it was discovered to have a heavy layer of grime. The second drive was in nearly as poor condition.

The cleaner the computer room, the better. You won't be able to eliminate all contaminants, but this isn't really necessary. Your goal is to reduce the number of contaminants.

To dust the outside surfaces of the computer equipment and surrounding countertops, use a cloth dampened with water or a mild cleaner. A damp cloth will pick up and trap the dust instead of spreading it around or tossing it into the air. Don't use anything like a feather duster anywhere near the computer. If you vacuum the floor, move the instrument slowly to keep down the amount of dust.

As electricity flows through the circuits, heat is generated inside the computer. If you put your hand over the ventilation slots on top of the main cabinet you'll feel the heat coming out, especially over the power supply.

If the heat is allowed to build up inside, some strange things can happen, such as unexplainable errors. If the heat buildup continues, actual damage can be done. Heat can also cause premature "aging" of the components, and will eventually increase the chances of malfunction or failure.

Recognizing that heat is a serious problem with circuits, the designers of the Macintosh wanted to make sure that the risk of heat damage was minimal. Consequently, the Macintosh is one of the coolest running computers of comparable power around. A cooling fan is not usually needed.

However, it is critical that you NEVER block the ventilation slots. Don't place papers or anything else on top of the computer. Keep the ventilation open and free. To further reduce the risk, never operate the computer in an overly warm room. Although the Macintosh is designed to tolerate any temperature from 50 degrees to 104 degrees, it is best to quit work if the room temperature is higher than about 85.

Although a cooling fan isn't a requirement, it can help, especially when the workroom is warm. The higher the surrounding temperature, the more important a cooling fan becomes.

FIG. 7–1 A cooling fan can also be installed inside the Macintosh and out of the way.

Typically, the cooling fan sits on top of the main unit. The better fans have a case that matches that of the Macintosh. The MacBCool from MPH Computer Products is one such device, and brings with it the additional advantage of a built-in surge protector and power switch. (This external power switch saves wear on the Mac's own, and difficult to replace, power switch.)

Be especially careful with the monitor screen. The nonglare coating can be damaged. (If you use a polarizing filter over the screen, use only lens cleaner and lens paper for cleaning the filter.)

Do not leave open containers near the computer. Be very careful about getting liquids of any kind into the electronics of the computer. Do not use a damp cloth inside anything electronic. Dust will have very little effect on the electronic components under normal use.

Cleaning the inside of the computer isn't really necessary, because the inside components aren't sensitive to dust as long as it is dry. (Even so, make it a habit to clean away any dust when you open the computer for other reasons.)

The internal parts of the printer are more sensitive to dust. Paper gives off a surprising amount of dust, which can jam the mechanical parts. Careful use of a vacuum cleaner with a soft brush attachment is usually the best way to tackle dust. Be extremely careful, though, to avoid damaging anything. And make sure you don't leave behind any hairs or fibers. NEVER stick your fingers inside unless the printer is unplugged from the outlet.

The computer (and many other devices) circulates air inside by convection for cooling purposes. As the warmer air rises and leaves the computer, outside air is drawn in. If there is dust or other contaminants in that air, it will also be drawn in. Dust may also enter the disk drives, the one spot where it can do the most damage. Although a little dust is unlikely to affect the circuits, it's murder on anything mechanical.

It's possible to filter the incoming air, but since this can reduce the amount of airflow, attaching filters to the ventilation slots is not advisable. (It's also not really necessary unless the enviMonment around the computer is usually bad, in which case you will probably want to find some other way to solve the dust problem.) A cooling fan can help increase the air flow. Never block the incoming air, even with thin filters, unless you have an auxiliary fan. Even then it's not a good idea.

Another part of the computer environment is the power that keeps it running. Power companies are well known for supplying "dirty" power (with surges, spikes and brown-outs). Although it isn't actually a maintenance step, using a line protector to keep these electrical transients out of the computer can be important in preventing damage to the delicate circuits.

If your area is prone to brown-outs (drops in line voltage) or regular and unpredictable power outages, you might also want to invest in a battery backup unit for your computer. These devices keep the power flowing at a

FIG. 7–2 A line protector for the computer.

steady level, even if the electricity coming into your home or office fluctuates or stops.

An uninterruptible power supply (called a UPS by some manufacturers) is important for any computer that is used in an area where the incoming power may suddenly and unexpectedly disappear. With the Macintosh, the need is even greater due to the way some programs save data to the diskette. When you open a file, the computer searches the directory track to find where on the diskette the data is stored. In a sense, this is like taking a file folder from a cabinet and leaving it open on the table. If a splash of water (power interruption) comes through, the file can be ruined.

If you don't have a UPS, and don't care to buy one, at the very least make it a practice to save your work to disk regularly. Some experts even suggest that you save the work, and then eject the diskette to make certain that the file has been closed and stored safely. Then insert the diskette again and go back to work. Now if the power fails, all you'll lose is the work you've done since the last save.

DRIVE HEAD CLEANING

There are two opinions about head cleaning. One is that it is never necessary and can only cause damage. The other is that you should clean the heads after every so many hours of use and that the cleaning will cause no damage at all.

Both are true, sort of. Obviously, you're better off leaving the heads alone as much as possible. But when cleaning is necessary, it has to be done.

Nor can you afford to wait until the recorded data is full of errors due to a dirty head.

Anything abrasive used on the heads is obviously capable of damaging the heads. The same goes for cleaning fluids that can affect other parts in the drive. If you stay with a well-known brand you should have no trouble at all.

The idea of cleaning the heads after so many hours can also be misleading. The key is your own environment. Obviously if you work in a sterile environment and use only the best quality diskettes, deposits will be minimal. You won't need to clean the heads very often. On the other hand, if you're a heavy smoker or have the computer in a dirty air environment (shame on you!), you will have to clean the heads more often.

Head cleaners can only take off "new" deposits. If you let those deposits build up over a long period of time, they become permanent parts of the heads. No cleaning kit in the world will take off such deposits, at least not without destroying the head at the same time.

There are various ways of cleaning the heads. Before people realized how much damage could be caused, abrasive cleaners were used. These literally scratched away the contaminants. Fortunately, very few of these are around now. Such a cleaner will certainly take away all the built-up grime. It will also take away the surface of the head.

The next step is a "nonabrasive" head cleaner with a bottle of fluid in the package. Generally such a package is less expensive and also tends to last

FIG. 7—3 Head cleaning kit.

longer. Again you have to be careful that the rotating pad is not too abrasive. (Stick with a reputable brand and you won't have much to worry about in this respect.)

Be careful not to oversoak or undersoak the pad. Both can cause problems. If the pad is undersoaked, the abrasive action is increased. (It also won't clean the head as well.) If it is made too wet, you'll have the excess fluid sloshing around inside the delicate parts of the drive. It will evaporate before too long, but in the meantime it can cause problems. Worse yet, there's no way to know if harmful materials have been deposited elsewhere in the drive or if other damage has been caused that will show up at a critical moment.

The most expensive head cleaners are presoaked with cleaner. Carefully measured amounts are already on the diskette cleaning pad, which means that there is virtually no risk of contaminated cleaning fluid dripping into places you don't want it. But they cost more to begin with and also wear out sooner. Since there is never an excess of cleaning fluid, the fluid will evaporate more quickly from the cleaning pad, making the diskette useless, if not dangerous. This won't happen if you follow the directions, though. The advantage is that you have much less risk of damaging the heads, the drive itself, or other diskettes you put in. Personally, I believe that this lower risk easily warrants the higher cost. The difference in price just isn't all that much.

Despite what you might read or hear elsewhere, *never* attempt to clean the heads by hand. First, you stand a good chance of knocking the heads out of alignment this way. Second, using something like a cotton swab can leave tiny threads behind which can cause all sorts of problems.

DISKETTES AND SOFTWARE

The more you use a diskette, the more chance there is of trouble. In Chapter 3 you learned how tough, and how delicate, a diskette is. The microfloppies used in the Macintosh are known as being the most reliable yet produced. But, even the best-made diskettes can present problems.

The major source of any difficulty is the allocation table or directory. Each time you use the diskette, the computer reads this track to learn what you have on the diskette. This means that the life of the diskette is directly proportional to the number of times you use this track.

The second major problem is that of editing. Changes in a diskette file can scatter that file all over the diskette. A disjointed file is much more prone to hand out errors than one that is in a logical sequence.

Think of it as several very long letters to friends, written over a period of a year or more. Before you send them you want everything to be just right. So you go back to the loose pages and add little notes. Over a period of time you have a massive stack of scribbles and pages. It would be almost impossible for you to keep track of which pages go to which friends.

The computer doesn't have quite this much trouble, but it still has to keep track of which changes you've made, and to which files. Those changes may end up scattered all over the diskette, and it could be like having a heavy wind get hold of those letter files.

The solution is to make copies often. You can copy a single file, a group of files, or all the files on a diskette. Complete instructions are in your user's manual. If you don't already know how to use the copying programs, take the time (*right now!*) to learn.

Programs used often should also be copied on a regular basis if the program allows this. Many don't in order to thwart software pirates. The new copy also has a new allocation track, which will bring a worn program back to life again.

If the program is "copy protected," you may be able to make a backup copy by using a program, such as MacSmith or Copy II Mac, that breaks through the protection schemes of "uncopyable" programs. The purpose of such copy programs is not to help software pirates but to allow legitimate users to backup their important (and expensive) originals.

Don't wait until the program or data diskette has failed before making the backup. Do so immediately! Right now, in fact. If you have diskettes that are used often that haven't been backed up recently, put down this book and do it—*now!* If the backup sits on the shelf or in the box for a year, great. You don't make the backup to use, you make it to ensure that a diskette failure doesn't knock you down and out.

Before filing away the backup copy for safekeeping, take a moment to test it. If it is a program, try it out. Don't just see if it will load—actually work it. If it is a data diskette, check it to see if the data has been transferred intact and without errors.

DIAGNOSTICS PROGRAMS

At the time of this writing, there are few diagnostics programs available for the Macintosh. Sooner or later, someone will make such a program commercially available. And when this happens, take the time to investigate it. In the meantime, readers of this book may be interested in the special offer described at the end of this section.

Some diagnostic programs check out the whole system, including the various circuits. Other programs test only parts of it, such as the RAM or ROM chips.

Those that check the circuitry should be capable of running the various tests a number of times, and selectable for the various kinds of tests. If there is a problem in RAM, for example, it may not show up in a single test. Quite often 30 or more cycles of testing are required, and there is probably no need to run 30 tests on the ROM or CPU at that time. However, since repair of the circuitry is generally handled by replacement of the entire board, testing the ROM, RAM, and CPU aren't necessarily useful for the average end user except as a means of periodically testing the component integrity (discussed below).

Many people buy a diagnostic package, and then think that it is useful only to spot problems after they have happened. Actually this is its least important use, as far as the computer owner is concerned.

Using a diagnostics package should be a part of your regular maintenance schedule. As mentioned, especially important are those programs that test the disk drives, since these are the most critical devices in your computer and the ones most prone to malfunction.

As mentioned in Chapter 2, the technical advisor on this book has designed a Macintosh diagnostics program. A special price is available for owners of this book. If you mention that you have gone out and bought a copy of this book with your order, the price for the program is $30 ($35 outside North America). Arizona residents must add an additional 6%, or $1.80. You must mention this book to get the discount.

Those interested can order the program from Tetra, P.O. Box 26275, Tempe, AZ 85282.

OTHER STEPS

It's all too easy to get used to the power of the computer and forget that it is quite delicate in certain ways. Each hour you spend with flawless operation tends to make you forget that things *can* go wrong, regardless of how well the computer is built.

Make it a habit each time you sit down to the computer to review in your mind all the things that can go wrong. Pay close attention to what it is doing and how things are working. The more you use a particular program or function, the more important this is.

If you have a friend with a Macintosh, sit down and use your friend's machine occasionally with your programs and data diskettes. Trade the opportunity and give your friend a session with your computer under the same conditions. This will tell both of you quite a bit about how well the computer system is functioning.

For example, if a diskette or program functions perfectly on your machine and not on the other, something is wrong with one of the two. Don't assume that the problem is with your friend's computer. Even if your own computer seems to be operating correctly, it could be having problems. For example, if the heads in your drive are misaligned, you'll be recording information that can only be read on a drive with heads that are misaligned in exactly the same way.

Such swapping of computer time will help to keep you informed of any serious malfunctions that are occurring, especially if you do it regularly. It gives you a basis for comparison that many people don't have.

If you don't have a friend with another Macintosh, contact your dealer.

Chances are he'll let you make use of one of the floor machines for a short time, especially if you've been a good customer.

An even better idea is to join a user's group. Other members in the group are likely to be after the same sort of cross checking. As you check your system, they are checking theirs. (You'll also end up with a valuable source of information, and plenty of new friends with your same interests.)

USER'S GROUPS

At first it may not seem that joining a user's group has much to do with maintenance or repair. Yet this can be a very important part of it all. Within the user's group you'll find others with a mutual interest—namely the Macintosh itself.

Some of the users will be inexperienced. Others will have enough knowledge to design and build their own computers. Quite a few are bound to have tips. What kinds of problems are common? What solutions have they found to those problems? Some user's groups even offer repair services and modifications at discounted prices to members.

A user's group also tends to have a wealth of public domain (free!) software available, much of which is for utility use. The first diagnostics routines, for example, are likely to crop up within user's groups. Quite often this free software is equal in quality to, and sometimes better than, commercial programs.

SUMMARY

There is very little maintenance to be done with your computer system. Invest just a few minutes per week and you've done just about everything necessary to keep your system running without trouble.

The environment around the system is critical. The cleaner you keep the general area, the fewer problems you'll have and the less maintenance you'll need. Keep dust and other contaminants away from the computer as much as possible.

If you ignore the drive heads for too long they could develop a permanent build-up of particles that no cleaner can remove. The result will be faulty reading and writing of data, at unpredictable times. A periodic cleaning of the heads, using the best quality head cleaning kit, will help to keep the heads working perfectly for many years. How often you clean the heads will be determined by how much your computer is used and how clean its surroundings are.

The most delicate part of a computer system is the software. Handle the diskettes carefully. Just as important, make backups of all diskettes a regular part of your work schedule. The cost of diskettes is cheap compared to the cost of replacing lost programs or data.

TABLE 7−1.
Maintenance Routine

Daily
1. Make backup copies of all data diskettes you've been using. This should be done at the end of each session and periodically during the session.

Weekly
1. Give the computer area a quick clean to cut down the amount of dust.
2. Make copies of all data diskettes that have been used heavily.
3. Clean disk drive heads, if needed.

Monthly
1. Thoroughly clean entire area, including the inside of the printer.
2. Clean disk drive heads.
3. Run a diagnostics program on your system.
4. Test devices and equipment that are rarely used.

Occasionally
1. Test backups already made, and rotate backups to keep the most current backup in use.
2. Make new backups of important programs and data, if needed.
3. Spend some time with your diskettes on someone else's Macintosh.
4. Learn something new about your system and its programs.

Table 7−1 is a guide to routine maintenance of your computer. The actual frequency of the maintenance routines will be determined by your usage of the system. For example, if you only work at the computer for a few hours per week you probably won't need to clean the drive heads as often. This listing is only a general guide. Set up a schedule for your own circumstances.

Chapter 8
Upgrading Your System

Just when you think you have everything you need as far as computers go, something else comes along. The printer you have may not be printing fast enough for your needs, or perhaps the character quality needs to be improved. You may decide that the built-in monitor isn't large enough and that you want an external monitor. There are a number of modifications that can be done to the hardware, and you're almost certain to be adding new software programs from time to time.

Even if you don't add something to your system, the day could easily come when an existing piece of equipment requires replacement. The steps in replacing a device are nearly the same as adding that device for the first time.

This chapter will show you how to handle some of the most common additions. Your own circumstances will be slightly different, depending on the equipment you're using. However, the general guidelines presented here should help.

When installing a new piece of equipment, try to change only one piece at a time. For example, if at all possible don't add a new printer *and* a new, untested printer cable at the same time.

It's important that you become familiar with the new device as soon as possible. If it has an installation manual with it (most accessories do), read it through carefully, cover to cover. Don't skim or skip. Certainly don't try to install it while reading the manual for the first time.

The biggest problem that most people have is that they're in too much of a hurry. That new drive you've been waiting for arrives and seems to cry out for immediate use. Off comes the cabinet and in goes the drive, with little more than a cursory glance at the manual. The result—the thing doesn't work.

Slow down. And then go slower yet. Take your time. If you don't understand the instructions, go back and read them again. Have a very good idea of

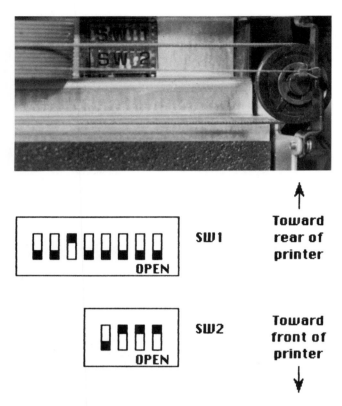

FIG. 8—1 The DIP switches of a printer.

what you're doing before you start and the installation is much more likely to be successful.

You'll actually save time—and much frustration—by taking the time to become familiar with the information first.

Before actually installing anything, go through the procedure at least once mentally. Do you know which steps to take and when?

Check and double check any switch settings or jumper changes you've had to make. If no switches are to be changed, be sure that you know this as well.

Finally, *never* install a device while power is flowing. Shut off the switch. To further protect yourself, unplug the computer. If you leave the computer plugged in, be aware that the line and power switch are still "hot."

REPLACING A DRIVE

The most delicate part of any computer system is the disk drive. Since it's mechanical, it gets more wear and tear than the nonmechanical parts (the electronic circuits). Sooner or later you'll have problems of one type or another with the drives.

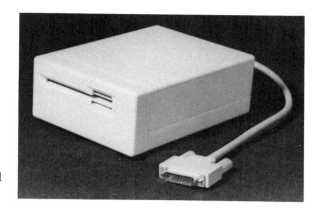

FIG. 8–2 The external drive.

Chapter 4 gives you detailed information on how to determine what the cause of the trouble is, and how to fix some of those problems. The steps from Chapter 7 are important for preventing those malfunctions *before* they happen. Even so, the day may come when you have to replace one of the drives.

Replacing an external drive is nothing more than unplugging the old one and plugging in the new. Even replacement of the internal drive is little more than a "plug 'n go" situation. Of course you have to open the case and remove a couple of screws, but there are no switches to set and no other complications.

At the time of this writing, only a few manufacturers supply disk drives for the Macintosh. More could come along, which means that it's also possible that installation of one of these "off brands" could be more difficult. As always, the manual that comes with the replacement should tell you what you need to know.

FIG. 8–3 Removing the cabinet.

FIG. 8—4 Inside the computer. Note drive case.

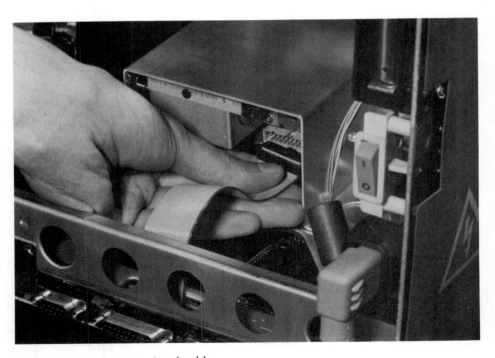

FIG. 8—5 Disconnect signal cable.

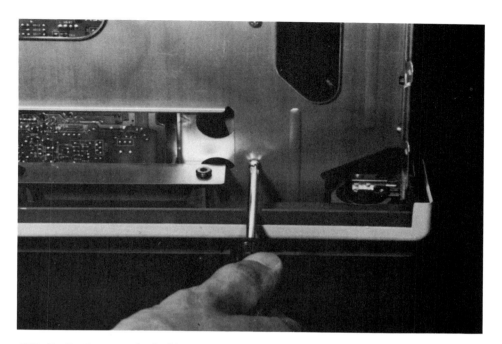

FIG. 8—6 Remove the holding screws.

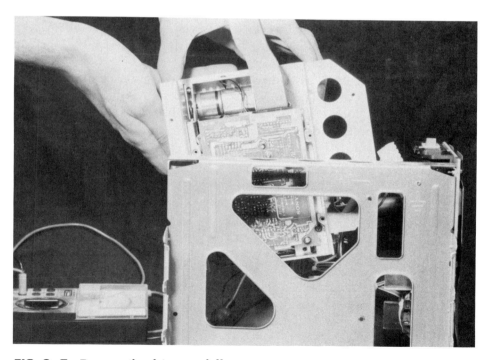

FIG. 8—7 Remove the drive carefully.

Whichever drive you use, there are certain replacement steps that are always the same. The power should be off, and preferably the power cord should be removed from the wall outlet.

Remove the cover by taking out the holding screws and popping the case. You can now access the holding screws of the drives. With the screws out, disconnect the main cable from the disk drive. After this, the drive slides out easily.

Replacement is the opposite. Just be sure that you have the connector in the proper orientation. Although it is keyed and difficult to connect improperly, there have been cases of people forcing the connector into place backwards, thus damaging the connector, the drive, and the computer.

HARD DRIVES

As with so many peripherals, you can't buy just any hard drive and expect it to work. Your job of installing the hard drive will be much simpler if you choose a unit that is designed to work with the Macintosh. Most of these are made specifically to be another of those "plug 'n go" situations. Installation of the new hard drive is generally as easy as plugging it in.

One of the greatest advantages of a hard drive is the increased speed of operation. This is especially important to those who have a 128K machine. Many programs are so large that they will be unable to fit into RAM. Instead, overlays are used within the program, telling the program to go back to the diskette when certain routines are needed. With a floppy drive system, this constant searching of the diskette can slow your operation down. A hard drive isn't a complete solution to the problem, but it will certainly speed up many operations and functions.

Unfortunately, most hard drives are limited by the communications protocol used by the Macintosh. This normally allows the hard drive to operate at speeds not much greater than that of the built-in or external disk drives. They are a little faster, however.

FIG. 8—8 A hard drive for the Macintosh. *Courtesy of Sunol Systems.*

FIG. 8—9 A Tecmar hard drive. *Courtesy of Tecmar, Inc.*

Even so, the most important advantage of having a hard drive is the capability of mass storage. You can squeeze anything from about 5 megabytes to more than 350 megabytes, depending on the type and size of hard drive used.

Most hard drives available for the Macintosh bring additional problems with them. Almost all require that you learn the new operating techniques required for that specific drive. Some are all too delicate and will scrap the files on the hard drive (all of them, at times) if you don't follow the procedure exactly.

For systems that allow more than one Macintosh connected, it's almost always best to set things up with just one Mac. Once this is up and working, proceed to linking in the other Macs on the overall system.

Be sure that you read through the instruction manual completely. Not doing so can cost you hours of wasted work, and possibly even an empty hard drive.

As with a drive swap, by paying attention to the various settings and connections and making sketches, you should have no problem getting the new unit to work. As mentioned at the beginning of this section, hooking a hard drive to your Macintosh is usually very simple. Getting the special operating system up and running is a little more complicated, and varies from brand to brand. The instructions that came with the new unit should tell you exactly what to do.

FIG. 8–10 Thanks to Sunol's Sun*Mac and its proprietary RLL (Run Length Limited) system, it's now possible to cram up to 368 megabytes of storage via linked hard drives. Courtesy of Sunol Systems.

PRINTERS

Printers come in two basic types, and in two basic configurations. The two types are dot matrix and those that use a wheel or ball (letter-quality printers). The two configurations are parallel and serial. A serial printer uses data that is sent one bit at a time. The parallel printer uses data that is sent one byte (eight bits) at a time. Each has advantages and disadvantages. With other computers, most people use the parallel configuration since this leaves open the serial connectors for other functions, such as modem communications. With the Macintosh, this isn't the case since the Macintosh doesn't have a parallel port.

However, the Macintosh does have available something very special called a LaserWriter. This printer can produce images that are almost indistinguishable from professional typesetting, and brings with it the extra ability of graphics that no typesetter can match.

At the moment, there aren't many printers that will interface with the Macintosh. Before you make the purchase, be sure that you have a written guarantee that you can return the printer if it doesn't work with your computer.

It's possible to use a software patch to help match certain printers to the Macintosh. One such program from Creighton Development, Inc. (4931 Birch, Newport Beach, CA 92660). This program, called ProPrint, is supposed to support a number of letter-quality printers. I haven't had the chance to test this program, but it is "Fully Warranteed."

If you stick to one of the few printers that are built strictly for the Macintosh, such as the ImageWriter or the LaserWriter, you'll have no problem. Installation is simply "plug 'n go." For any other printer, you may have to make some modifications, and you may not be able to get the printer to work at all.

Cabling is the biggest consideration when installing a printer. Building a cable isn't that complicated, especially for the Macintosh. (Fewer pins are

FIG. 8—11 The LaserWriter from Apple. *Courtesy of Apple Computer, Inc.*

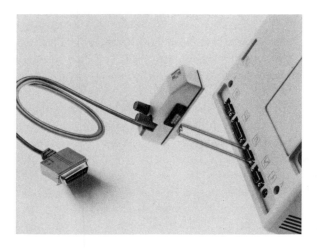

FIG. 8–12 The Mac-Port-Adaptor makes it possible to connect many printers that wouldn't otherwise be compatible with the Macintosh. *Courtesy of Assimilation.*

used. The ImageWriter, for example, uses only four pins on the Macintosh side, and only five at the printer.) The manual that came with your printer will generally tell which pins are used for which function. Below you will find a chart for the serial printer port of the Macintosh. If you're lucky, all you have to do is to match these to the printer. (Don't forget to test the cable for continuity.)

Before even attempting to make any connections, get out the manual for your printer and read it cover to cover. Become familiar with the operations, options, switch settings and so forth. The more you know, the better.

TABLE 8–1. Serial (Data) Pin Allocations

Pin	Use	Pin	Use
1	Ground	6	Data set ready
2	Transmit data	7	Signal ground
3	Receive data	8	Data carrier detect
4	Request to send	9–19	Not used
5	Clear to send	20	Data terminal ready

TABLE 8–2.
Centronix Parallel Pin Allocations

Pin	Use	Pin	Use
1	Strobe	10	Not used
2	Data bit 0	11	Busy
3	Data bit 1	12–15	Not used
4	Data bit 2	16–17	Ground
5	Data bit 3	18	Not used
6	Data bit 4	19–30	Ground
7	Data bit 5	31–32	Not used
8	Data bit 6	33	Ground
9	Data bit 7	34–36	Not used

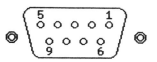

Serial Connectors

1. Ground
2. +5VDC
3. Ground
4. Transmit Data +
5. Transmit Data –
6. +12VDC
7. $\overline{CTS}$/External clock
8. Receive Data +
9. Receive Data –

FIG. 8—13 The Macintosh RS-422 serial data connector and pin locations.

Mac ImageWriter cable

Mac DB-9   **ImageWriter DB-25**

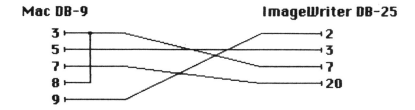

**All pins not shown are not present
or have no connection**

FIG. 8—14 ImageWriter pin allocations.

**DB-25 Connector
(common on modems)**

FIG. 8—15 Standard (RS-232) serial data connector and pin locations.

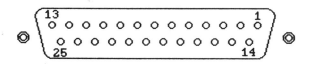

Centronics parallel interface

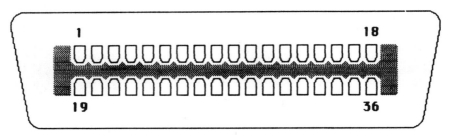

FIG. 8—16 A parallel (Centronics) connector and pin locations.

Visually inspect the printer. Locate the controls and learn how to use them—even if you don't think you'll need those options. Also look at the print head. Some are tied in place to reduce damage in shipping. Others may be packed along the sides.

As with many computer devices, printers often have DIP switches to set. Many printers are designed to accommodate a variety of computers. The switches allow you to configure the printer to your needs. The switches may also set other functions of the printer. The printer manual is your guide in all this. You may not have to change them, but the only way to know is to read *that manual*.

Don't forget to shut down the power before changing any of the DIP switch settings. Most printers won't recognize switch setting changes while power flows. Others can be permanently damaged.

The manual that came with the printer should tell you everything you need to know about the switch settings. Read it carefully. You can't damage anything by not having the correct settings, but the operation of the printer won't be right, if it works at all.

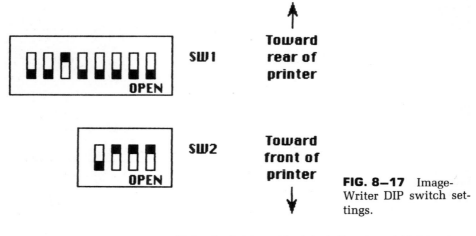

FIG. 8—17 Image-Writer DIP switch settings.

FIG. 8–18 An Apple modem for the Macintosh. *Courtesy of Apple Computer, Inc.*

MODEMS

There are two basic types of modem presently available, internal and external. Only the external type will work with the Macintosh at this time. The day may come, however, when an internal modem conversion will be made available, and a short discussion of the advantages and disadvantages of each might be in order.

An external modem has the advantage of being "portable." You can move it from computer to computer by merely changing the cables from one computer to the other. Also, the controls are on the modem, making it easier to handle and monitor. At the same time, it gives you one more thing to carry around if you move the computer from place to place, and one more thing to take up space on the work table.

FIG. 8–19 The complete Macintosh system. Note the modem tucked beneath the telephone. *Courtesy of Apple Computer, Inc.*

The internal modem has an advantage in that it is tucked away inside the computer. That saves on desk space and on the number of items to be moved. It also generally reduces the amount of control you have on the modem.

An external modem can be "direct connect" or "acoustic." The acoustic modems are very inexpensive and have been in use for many years, but they are now essentially obsolete. These modems have a cradle for the telephone. The circuitry generates "beeps" to represent the data, which is picked up by the telephone in the same way as it picks up your voice and other sounds.

An acoustic modem has a severe disadvantage, however. As it picks up the beeps that are the data, it can also pick up any other sounds in the room. This can produce garbled or unusable data on the other end. The worse the fit of the telephone receiver into the cradle, the more garbage it will pick up from the room.

Direct-connect modems eliminate this problem and are generally to be preferred. A line connects the modem directly to the telephone outlet in the wall. No external sounds can invade. However, this increased reliability costs money.

Modems come in two common speeds: 300 and 1200 baud, with one baud being approximately one bit per second. For example, a 300-baud modem will transmit and receive data at 300 bits per second. The 1200-baud modem is four times faster, making it generally better (also much more expensive). Becoming more popular are modems capable of 2400 baud and even higher.

Many modems that handle 1200 baud can be switched to handle slower speeds. With them you can communicate with other computers that have only the slower models. A modem that cannot make this change will only save you $150 (or less). You *cannot* make a 300-baud modem run at 1200.

The usual upper limit for reliability across standard telephone lines is 2400 baud. Transmission and reception of data at speeds higher than this could mean that the data will be garbled, and often unusable.

If you're planning to hook up a modem, there is an excellent book you can use for more information about modems, installing serial peripherals, and direct computer-to-computer communications links. It is *Increasing Your Business Effectiveness Through Computer Communications*, written by Phillip Good, and published by Chilton Book Company.

RAM UPGRADES

If you have the standard version of the Macintosh, the main board will have 128K in RAM. If you need more memory (and who doesn't), it is possible to upgrade the system to 512K and more. Upgrades to 512K are fairly standard. A few companies also offer an upgrade to a full megabyte (1000K) in RAM. (See Appendix C on 1 megabyte upgrades.)

More and more programs that require more RAM are being made available. This is a trend that is bound to continue. The additional RAM can also be used as a RAM disk—a section of RAM that pretends to be a disk drive. (To do this, you'll need sufficient RAM and a program that will set up a RAM disk.) Access to data in a RAM disk is incredibly fast.

The best way to handle the upgrade is to let someone else who knows how to do it handle the job. There are a number of companies around the country that specialize in this upgrade. The cost is generally quite reasonable. A users' group in your area may also offer this upgrade, with a discount for group members.

The advantage in having one of the companies perform the work is that the job is guaranteed. If the person doing the upgrade does not offer a guarantee, go elsewhere.

The upgrade requires soldering and some components. Much of the soldering is done on the chips, particularly the new RAM chips. If you're unfamiliar with soldering, you may well ruin both the chips and the entire main board. This is an expensive way to learn that there are times when a job is best left to a professional.

There are bound to be a few readers, however, who have the technical expertise to successfully perform a RAM upgrade. To be perfectly honest, the number will be very small. Everyone else should skip the rest of this section.

The chances of destroying your computer while making the upgrade are very high. You can ruin the new RAM chips all too easily. Worse yet, you can turn the main digital board into a pile of very expensive junk in seconds. Under these circumstances it will have no trade-in value. In fact, even if you don't destroy the board, the modification will void any warranties, and will probably make it impossible for you to get a trade-in value.

To make up for any mistakes, you'll pay the full price of a brand new board. So, in a very real sense, you're gambling $1000 to possibly gain $100—and if you lose you'll be right back where you started and will *still* have to pay for the upgrade. Odds of 10 to 1 against you aren't exactly desirable.

If all that hasn't scared you away, proceed at your own risk.

The new RAM chips are of the 41256 variety. You'll need sixteen of them. To play it safe, you'll also need sixteen 16-pin sockets to hold the chips. You'll also need a dual 4:1 multiplexer, such as the Motorola SN74AS253N and another 16-pin socket for this chip. (This chip is a part of the new RAM select and access.) Two resistors will be needed. One of them can have a range anywhere within about 50% up or down from 3K. The other is a 47-ohm resistor. Both can have a ¼ watt rating.

You'll also need a top-quality, low-power, soldering tool and a desoldering tool. A wire cutter and needlenose pliers make the job easier and safer.

Remove the case and the main digital board. Find the section of the board where the RAM chips are located, and make a quick sketch of the correct polarity of the chips. Also locate the existing 74F253 chip (located at

F3) and the seven solder points next to the CPU toward the left side of the computer, and with pin 1 being closest to the front.

Next, clip all sixteen existing RAM chips. This destroys them, so there's no backing out. But, by clipping them, you reduce the danger to the board.

Very carefully, heat, desolder, and remove all the pins. (There will be 256 of them.) Be sure that the holes are open and clean. A toothpick can help open stubborn holes. Also check what you've done to be sure that you haven't created a solder bridge or caused other damage. It also helps to give the solder holes and board a gentle cleaning with an electronic degreaser.

Now install the sockets in the empty holes, and very carefully solder them into place. It's easy to get into a rush. Soldering 256 pins into place can be a tedious job. But rushing can cause either damage or a cold solder joint. Take your time and do the job right the first time.

Most sources suggest that you install the new chips and test the system at this point. That's a good idea and can help you to spot any errors you've made so far. The computer will still operate as a 128K machine, but if it doesn't operate correctly, you know that you've already messed things up or have a bad RAM chip.

The next step is more complicated. The SN74AS253 (or comparable) chip won't quite do the job itself. It must be modified to work correctly. For safety, and for ease in doing the job, the modifications can be done on the socket. Keep in mind that the chip has to fit into the socket, and that the socket has to fit into the board on top of the existing chip.

Solder the larger (3K or so) resistor between pins 15 and 16 on the socket. With a small gauge wire, solder together pins 3, 4, and 15. With the same wire, solder together pins 1, 8, 10, 11, 12, and 13.

Pins 2, 7, 14, and 16 get soldered directly to the same pins on the existing 74F253 chip (located at the coordinates of F and 3 on the main digital board). All other pins should be bent outwards and away from the socket to prevent them from making contact.

Now locate the seven solder points by the CPU. Pin 1 is closest to the front of the computer. It would be beneficial at this point to mark the pins on both the front and back of the board.

Solder the 47-ohm resistor between pin 7 of the new socket and pin 2 of the 7-point strip on the digital board. Next solder a small wire between 5 of the new socket and pin 3 of the solder points; and another wire between pin 6 on the socket to pin 6 on the strip.

Turn the board over and carefully cut the etched connection between pins 1 and 2 of that 7-point string near the CPU.

For newer 128K boards, things are slightly easier. For this you'll need two 2.2K resistors (installed at R40 and R41), and a 47-ohm resistor soldered across the R42 position. The new 74AS253N chip goes into the existing socket (located at the coordinates of G and 13 on the main board). In addition, a .1uf has to be soldered across C51. All that's left then is to make a cut across the etching W1, which says "128K only" next to it.

Assuming that you've done everything correctly, and that all the chips and resistors are good, you'll now have a 512K "Fat Mac."

Once again, it's *far* better to leave this modification to someone who is willing to offer at least a 90-day warranty on the work. After you've paid for the new RAM chips, the 74F253N chip, the sockets and resistors, you're actually only about $100 (tops) ahead. And this assumes that you can get a good price on the materials and have all the needed equipment on hand.

In my opinion, it's simply not worth the bother and risk. Let someone else handle the job who is willing to guarantee that the job will work, without damage to that expensive board.

COOLING FANS

Although the Macintosh is designed to operate cool without a cooling fan, it never hurts to provide this extra circulation. Heat buildup, even if small, can damage or age electronic components. Put your hand over the top of the computer after it has been in operation for a while and you'll feel the heat coming out. The more heat you can keep out of the Macintosh, the better.

Several companies offer cooling fans that sit on top of the Macintosh. Some of these also have built-in power switches, line filters, etc. that greatly add to their value.

You can also install the fan inside the Macintosh and out of the way. One company in Mesa, Arizona offers a do-it-yourself kit for $45 (including packing, shipping, and complete instructions on how to go about installation of the fan). This kit can be ordered from MacCOOLER, Design Eight, 1061 E. Hope St., Mesa, AZ 85203.

Whether you buy a premade unit, a kit, or attempt to install your own fan (it's not difficult), it's generally best to use a fan driven by standard 115-volt AC power. These fans are usually quieter than the DC models and seem to last longer. They're also often less expensive. In addition, having the fan wired to the incoming AC line voltage gives you a quick and easy way to know if power is getting to the computer.

EXTERNAL ACCESSORIES

The Macintosh is designed to operate "as is." There are no expansion slots for additional circuit boards. But there *are* some things that can be done to enhance your computer. These enhancements have found great popularity with computer users because of the increased power and versatility available. Print spoolers and RAM disks, for example, are wonderful features to have.

Assimilation, a California company, has made it possible to connect a variety of devices to the Macintosh. A port adaptor makes it possible to hook up many externals that require a standard parallel connector. Another device, called Mac-Turbo-Touch, gives the operator a numeric keypad for eas-

FIG. 8–20 Mac-Turbo-Touch accessory. *Courtesy of Assimilation.*

ier entry of numbers, and the option of a gyroscopic ball to replace the mouse. Still another product from Assimilation makes it possible to connect the Macintosh to a digital music synthesizer, for those who like to mix Bach with Mac.

As always, begin by reading through the instructions completely. Don't skim past sections just because you think you won't be needing them. There's no such thing as knowing too much about the device and its features.

If you're not careful when installing an accessory, you can run into all sorts of problems. If the installation requires soldering or other physical changes to the main computer circuits, there is always the chance of causing damage. There could also be electronic conflicts between the computer's circuits and those of the new board.

If your system functioned perfectly before the installation, and suddenly something isn't working any more, chances are good that you've done some-

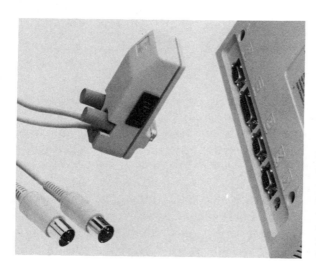

FIG. 8–21 Another interesting device, the MIDI-Conductor, makes it possible to connect your Macintosh to a digital audio synthesizer for some interesting computer music. *Courtesy of Assimilation.*

thing wrong, have missed a switch setting, or are trying to get the computer to do something it can't.

The software and hardware documentation should give you all the information you need as to what the board requires as far as installation and operation. Check both carefully.

It's possible that the board you choose will not be compatible with your system or with certain devices in your system. The dealer should be able to tell you what you need to know about compatibility. (The easiest way to avoid this problem is to use only products that have been proven to be fully compatible.)

SOFTWARE

Although the programs you use are not actually devices, there is often an installation procedure to follow. The manual that comes with the software should give you all the information you need to get the program up and working.

Just as you should when installing any other accessory, read through the manual before beginning. At least go through the installation section thoroughly. Despite what it seems at times, all the information you need is there (*if* you can understand it).

Some software is designed to work on a variety of computers, with modifications made to the software to get it to work on a specific computer. Sometimes the manual itself will not be specific to the computer. It might contain several sections, each for a different computer. If this is the case, be sure that you're using the instructions for your Macintosh.

If the program allows it, make at least one backup copy (preferably two) before you begin. Then if you make a mistake you're safe. I know one person who bought an expensive piece of software and didn't follow this simple rule. He was certain that he knew what to do, ". . . and besides, I'm following the instructions carefully." Within a few minutes that expensive software was a blank diskette.

VIDEO DIGITIZERS

One of the most interesting items available for the Macintosh is one that makes it possible to turn an existing image into something the computer can understand and use. Take a photograph or drawing, let the digitizer convert it, and you end up with the same image stored inside the Macintosh or on disk. After this, you can manipulate and/or print it as you need.

There are two basic ways to do this. One is to use what is called a solid state camera, such as MicronEye. These devices use a special kind of chip with optical properties. The MicronEye, for example, uses an IS32 Optic-RAM chip to work its magic. The actual image is "seen" by the optical chip

FIG. 8–22 The MicronEye solid state camera. *Courtesy of Micron Technology, Inc.*

and is then changed into black and white data, which registers in the computer as the digital values of 0 and 1 respectively.

Installation is simple. Plug the MicronEye system (camera and TTL board) into the modem port of your Macintosh (*with the power off*), insert the operating program, and you're ready to go.

Thunderware, Inc. has come up with a unique solution for digitizing images. The unit is called ThunderScan. The system consists of software, adaptor box, and a scanner cartridge that fits onto your ImageWriter. (Also supplied are white timing strips that can be attached to the platen that can speed up the scanning rate, and a special cover for the printer.) The adaptor box plugs into the Macintosh at the printer port, with the ImageWriter connected to the other side of the box. The scanner cartridge is already wired to the box. Replace the ribbon cartridge in your ImageWriter with this special cartridge, and you're ready to load in the software. (As always, shut off all power before making any connections or disconnections.)

MISCELLANEOUS

There is very little that the Macintosh can't do all by itself. If you install the proper devices and use the right software, it has astounding power unavailable from almost any other computer with comparable price and RAM. It can

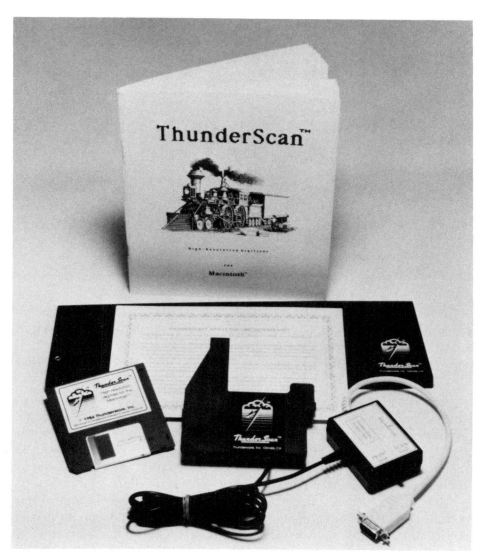

FIG. 8—23 ThunderScan turns your ImageWriter into an image digitizer. *Courtesy of Thunderware, Inc.*

be made to pretend to be a different computer by using an emulation package. (One accessory package, for example, makes it possible for your Mac to pretend to be an IBM PC.) It can communicate with other computers with the use of a modem, or directly with other Macintoshes.

Installation of some accessories is as easy as attaching a cable. Others require major changes to the hardware, or special patches to the software (either to the software that comes with the device, to the operating system, or possibly to both). A few devices require custom software to get them to go.

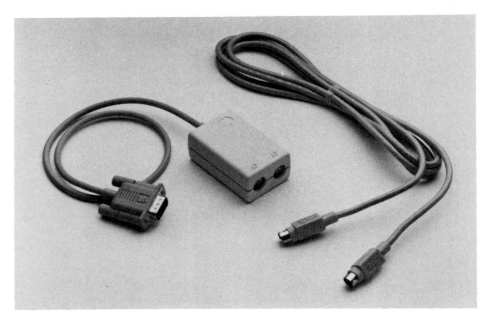

FIG. 8—24 Apple's own AppleTalk Personal Network allows you to connect up to 32 Macs together. *Courtesy of Apple Computer, Inc.*

The dealer should be able to inform you of the difficulty of installing a particular device you want to purchase. Buy it from him and he takes on the responsibility of providing you with everything you need for proper operation. A part of the sale is to provide to the customer (free or at a reasonable price) the initial assistance needed for the installation, special software or software patching programs, and whatever else is needed.

Magazines such as "MacWorld" and "Macazine" describe a wealth of modifications that can be done to your computer. If you decide to make a modification, be sure that you fully understand what it is that you are about to do, and the consequences if you make a mistake. Take a long, realistic look at your personal abilities before jumping into a project.

SUMMARY

Adding options and devices to your system is sometimes as simple as plugging a cable from the device to the back of the computer. Other times it requires that you open the computer and make some physical changes to the existing circuitry.

Before making the purchase you should have some idea of just how difficult it is to handle the installation, and if you have the knowledge, skills, and equipment needed. If a more permanent modification is required, are you willing to make this kind of change to your system? Or to go through the bother of changing things back later?

Before beginning the actual installation, read through the instructions completely. Then go through the steps of installation in your head. Do you understand what to do, when, and why?

Before giving up, read through the instructions again. Most of the time the information you need is right there—if you take the time to dig it out.

Chapter 9
Dealing with the Technician

No matter how well you maintain your computer or how much you learn about repairing it, sometimes you will have no choice but to call in a professional (and pay those professional fees!). It can't be helped. Certain repairs demand the use of special, expensive equipment. Others require special knowledge that is far beyond the scope of any single book.

This book is meant to reduce to a minimum those times when you have to hire a professional and to cut the amount you'll have to spend when those times occur. When you consult a professional you will already have taken care of many of the steps of diagnosis and will be able to supply a great deal of information to the technician. Since you've spent the time, he or she doesn't have to (and you don't have to pay for the time).

This book can go a long way toward reducing costs, but it can't reduce costs to zero.

MAIL ORDER

If you purchase through the mail, the situation is different. Very few mail order companies are set up to handle questions or problems. You get a discount price but are expected to take care of everything by yourself. The only responsibility that many mail order companies accept is to make sure the equipment is "as advertised." While they do guarantee that the equipment will arrive in good condition, they usually assume that the buyer knows enough to get the equipment or software functioning.

There is nothing dishonest in this; mail order companies simply aren't set up in the same way as a local dealer. They don't have the technical staff on hand to take care of questions and problems. Their basic job is to fill your order, which they usually do quite well.

If you know for certain that you can handle any problems with the installation and that you can wait for the delivery (and the delivery of the exchange if this is needed), mail order can save you some money.

If you have any doubts about your technical knowledge, you are probably better off working with a local dealer.

RESPONSIBILITIES OF THE DEALER

When selling you equipment or software, the dealer assumes a certain amount of responsibility. (If the dealer doesn't, you should probably find another.) The first dealer responsibility is to make sure that the computer is functioning when you get it. If you're buying an entire system, the dealer should see that everything functions as a unit before turning it over to you. It should not be handed over as nothing more than a pile of boxes. If the dealer operates this way, you might as well go through a mail order company and save some money. Insist that the product support promises are put in writing.

Many dealers include training in the purchase price. This training isn't meant to make you a computer expert. That takes years of work. The purpose of this training is to get you familiar with the computer and the software.

Occasionally the dealer will charge a small fee for this training. This is often true for instruction in how to operate a complicated piece of software. Even a $500 software program doesn't automatically bring with it a complete course. The more training you need, the higher the cost.

After the sale of hardware or software, the dealer continues to have the responsibility of customer care. If you have a problem a few weeks or months after getting the equipment home, you should feel welcome to call with questions. Service should continue beyond the warranty period.

Manufacturers of both hardware and software are famous for refusing to talk to the end user. They usually assume that end-user dealings are the responsibility of the person who sold you the item. Thus, even if it is not wanted, the responsibility often falls on the dealer to provide customers with the needed information.

People who are new to computing (about 75% of the dealer's sales) won't know what questions to ask when they make a purchase. Something as simple as formatting a diskette is a major accomplishment for some newcomers. The more the buyer works with the computer, the more questions he or she will have. After a short time certain questions and problems are bound to come up.

The dealer should provide competent technical assistance after the sale. The user needs a source of information when something goes wrong. This includes both technical questions involving operation of the software and hardware purchased, and repair when something goes wrong.

Simple questions should be without charge (if you're a customer). Questions that involve some instruction or other lengthy personal attention will probably require a fee. Repairs of any size will cost unless you're under warranty or have a service contract (which also costs).

Some dealers work on a smaller basis and do not keep a technical staff in the shop. If this is the case, the dealer should at least be able to guide you to the proper people or find the answers to your questions. Being small is no excuse for being unable to provide customer service when it is needed. Customer service is the responsibility of dealers of any size and something you should look for when choosing a dealer.

YOUR RESPONSIBILITIES

If you expect assistance or information from a local dealer begin by giving that dealer some business. If you bought your computer through the mail, don't expect the local dealer to answer all your questions and take care of all your problems free of charge.

Even if you didn't purchase your system from a particular dealer, you can build a working relationship by giving the company your other business. The next time you're in the market for a printer or some software, stop in and see the dealer you plan to use for help. You might have been thinking about getting some training on how to operate one of your programs. Perhaps the dealer has a course available.

THE TECHNICIAN

With the information in this book, you should be able to provide a considerable amount of information to the technician. Your goals are to reduce the cost of repair and the amount of time that repair will take. You'll be gaining a secondary benefit in that you'll be letting the technical staff know that you have some idea of what you're talking about.

Before even calling, try to find out if the malfunction has been caused by operator error. Unfortunately, the technician is probably used to dealing with customers who haven't even bothered to read the instruction manual.

The more accurate the information you provide, the easier the job of the technician. To you this means increased efficiency, lower cost, and less downtime with your computer sitting on the testing bench.

If the technician (and the shop) is honest and reliable, just the idea that they're dealing with someone intelligent will help. If the shop happens to be one of the very few dishonest ones around, the fact that you know a little something can deter the technician from trying to pull a fast one.

If you're observant you can tell quite a bit about how well the technician "knows his stuff" even over the phone. His or her responses to your information should make sense. (At the same time, a response of "I can't tell without looking at it" is often legitimate. The technician should be able to answer your questions without tossing around unnecessary technical jargon. If you have any qualms about the technician's qualifications, ask.

Don't be afraid to make suggestions or helpful comments. It's possible that you know something special about the circumstances. If you've gathered information (perhaps from the tests you've performed from this book), offer it. Anything that makes the technician's job easier will be appreciated. And it may also help reduce the amount you pay for the technical work.

TERMS OF REPAIR

Two-way communication is important in any transaction. Both parties should understand fully what is promised and what is expected before things begin. Misunderstandings can come up all too easily unless anticipated before things start.

You should have some idea of the terms and the cost before the work begins. The shop may not be able to give you an exact price until they've found the problem. (For example, a problem that you think is something minor in the disk drive might be something major on the system board.)

An experienced technician will usually be able to give you a fairly accurate estimate. This should be given to you in writing before the actual work begins. If further testing and diagnosis reveal that the problem is something more expensive, be sure to have it (in writing) that the dealer will call you before going ahead (unless you are not concerned about the expense).

Along with the price estimate you should have a time estimate. How long will your computer be tied up? If it goes beyond this period can you get a "loaner" or at least rent a machine to use while you're waiting?

What kind of warranty is given with the work? It should be *at least* 30 days on both parts and labor (90 days is better). Having the warranty in writing is important.

When the work is completed, ask for an itemized bill. This is your protection for any warranty service and is also a good thing to have around for future reference. To avoid complications, request the itemized list before the work begins. Some shops automatically keep itemized lists. Others don't.

Before turning over the computer, be sure the technician knows as much as possible about the problem and the symptoms. The more information you provide, the better.

Communication is important if you wish maximum efficiency and a good repair job.

SOLVING PROBLEMS

No matter how good the technician or how reputable the company, problems may arise. Many can be prevented if communication between you and the shop is carried on properly to begin with. Others result from unforeseen malfunctions, such as a faulty part. Occasionally a mistake is made during repair.

If the work is not done to your satisfaction, say so. But keep in mind that the nastier you are, the less willing they'll be to take care of the problem.

Talk first to the technician who did the work. Chances are the problem is something he or she can handle. If not, go to the service manager and then to the general manager. It might take a little longer to go through the chain of command, but the end results are often better.

SUMMARY

Before making a purchase, determine whether you'll be able to handle the installation alone, without the advice of a local dealer. If so, you can save money by using a mail order company. If you have doubts, you might be better off going with a local dealer.

Both the dealer and you have responsibilities. It's a two-way street—or should be. The dealer owes the customers all the necessary support for whatever is being sold and should be willing to stand behind the products carried. The staff should be competent enough to give sensible advice on which products will best suit your needs.

Chapter 10
Troubleshooting Guide

Finding the source of a malfunction isn't as difficult as you may think. It is nothing more than a logical process of elimination.

For example, assume that the computer or peripheral is completely dead. If the wall outlet is good, then the problem is definitely with the device. By checking the power supply (see Chapter 6), you'll have eliminated as the cause either the power-handling circuitry or the rest of the computer. Continue this process and eventually you'll have located the offending module.

Begin *always* with a check of the obvious. Is the computer plugged in? Is the wall outlet good? You'll find that the majority of malfunctions are a result of something easily rectified.

The symptoms will help to guide you to the source of the trouble. There are just so many things that can cause a particular malfunction. If a program refuses to load but everything else seems functional, the symptoms indicate that the most likely problem is with either the software or the drive (Chapters 3 and 4). Less likely, but possible, are things related to the drive. The power supply might not be providing sufficient power for the drive to operate properly (easily checked by testing the input to the drives). The program goes from the drive and into RAM memory, which means that a faulty loading can be a result of a RAM failure.

Quite often, what seems to be a major failure was brought about by something temporary, such as a surge or spike coming into the computer at just the wrong time. Turn the machine off for a few seconds and try again.

A troubleshooting guide, such as the one below, is just a quick guide to give you a starting place for diagnostics. Keep in mind that a troubleshooting guide is only the beginning of complete diagnostics. Sometimes the problem will be found quickly, using nothing more than the troubleshooting guide. Other times more complicated steps are needed (see Chapter 2).

TABLE 10—1. Troubleshooting Table

Symptom	Possible Problem	Cure	Chapter
Nothing happens	No power	Check cord, switch fuse	2,6
	Power supply	Check power supply	6
		Check connectors	2,5
	Main board	Check mainboard	2,5
Fuse blows often	Power supply	Check power supply	6
	Cabling	Check all cables	
	Main board	Check main board	5
	Other boards	Check (if possible)	6
Bell does not beep	Bad speaker or connector	Replace speaker or connector	
	Bad analog board		
	Bad main board	Replace main board	5
No display or poor display	Controls	Adjust controls	2,6
	No signal to video board	Check cables	6
	No power to video board	Check power	6
	Monitor	Check monitor	6
	Main board	Check main board	5
Drive LEDs do not come on	Bad or loose connector	Check or replace	4
	No power to drives	Check power	4,6
	Disk drive bad	Check disk drive	4
	Drive controller chip bad	Replace	4
	Main board	Check main board	5
Keyboard does not work	Keyboard not plugged in	Plug it in	
	Keyboard faulty	Check keyboard	6
	Keyboard cable or connector	Test cable or connector	6
	Main board bad	Check main board	5
Cannot load in programs; other program problems	Something silly	Check the obvious	
	Bad diskette	Try backup	
	No system on diskette	Use system diskette	
	Drive not working	Check drive	4
	Drive cable or connector	Check drive cable and connector	4
	RAM memory	Check and replace if necessary	5,6
	Main board	Check main board	5
	Drive heads	Clean or replace	4

Symptom	Possible Problem	Cure	Chapter
Lines or patterns on screen	Bad diskette	Try a backup	3,4
	Video circuits bad	Check analog board	6
Mouse does not work	Something silly	Check connections	6
	Mouse dirty	Clean	6,7
	Diskette bad	Try a backup	3
	Mouse malfunction	Replace	6
Printer problems	Something silly	Check the obvious	6,8
	No output from computer	Check cable	6
		Check connector	6
		Check main board	5
	Printer	Check printer	6,8
Hard drive problems	Cables	Check cables	4,8
	Main board	Check main board	5
	Hard drive	Replace	8
Blinking "X" on screen	No system on diskette		3,4
Mouse does not roll	Dirty roller or contacts	Clean mouse	6
	Mouse bad	Replace mouse	6
Printer failure	Bad cable or connectors	Check cable and connectors	6
	No power to printer	Check power	2,6
	DIP switches not set	Set switches	
	Incompatible printer	Use another printer	
No time, date or inconsistent	Dead clock battery	Replace battery	

TABLE 10–2.
The Opening Screen Icons

Icon	Meaning
Happy face	Everything is fine
Sad face	Possible hardware problem; the computer is unable to continue.
X	Possible damage to diskette, or program malfunction.
?	Computer is waiting for a diskette to be inserted, or doesn't recognize that one is in place.
Clock	Wait—program is loading or command is being carried out.

Appendix A
Making a Case Popper

There are a number of ways to open the case of the Macintosh. One is to find a dealer who will sell you the official tool for splitting the case open. Another is to pry against the case with various things until it lets go—sometimes in pieces. Both methods can be expensive.

If you plan to get inside your Macintosh, it's a worthwhile investment to get a case popper. But, instead of spending all the time and money to find and buy one, why not spend less time and money and make your own?

It's not difficult to do. The instructions below tell you exactly how to go about it. What we've shown is one of the least expensive means possible, and one with a built-in joke—"the key to the Macintosh." It also costs less than a dollar, and takes about 10 minutes, to make.

If you don't care to make this particular type, you can build one out of any number of materials. There are a few things to keep in mind when designing a case popper, though.

The case popper is meant to fit into the small crack between the front and back parts of the case. Pressure will be applied in two directions in order to separate the case. Since the case is made of plastic, a wide blade is needed to distribute the force and reduce the danger of digging into the plastic.

To further reduce damage, the tool should push only in straight lines. One blade pushes straight forward, while the other pushes straight back. *Do not use a twisting motion*, since this defeats the purpose of the wide blades and also increases the chance of damaging the case.

Brass parts were chosen as the material for several reasons. One is that brass resists corrosion. Even more important, it accepts solder readily, which makes joining the parts easy. (Other kinds of keys will not work as well, if at all.)

The hinge is used for the two prying blades. A small hinge (brass) was picked. A larger hinge can be used if you wish, but the hinge sides must be thin enough so they will fit into the crack of the case. Before you put yourself

Materials List

small brass hinge   torch
2 brass keys   vise grips or pliers
solder   vise or "helping hands"

through a lot of effort, fold the hinge and put it into the crack. This will tell you if the hinge you've picked out will work. It will also tell you where to place the two keys on the hinge so that the keys do not get in the way.

The first step is to bend the two keys slightly. This can be done by holding the blade of the key with a pliers or vise grips, or by placing it into a vise. Push gently to keep control of the bending. Try to get both keys bent with the same curve.

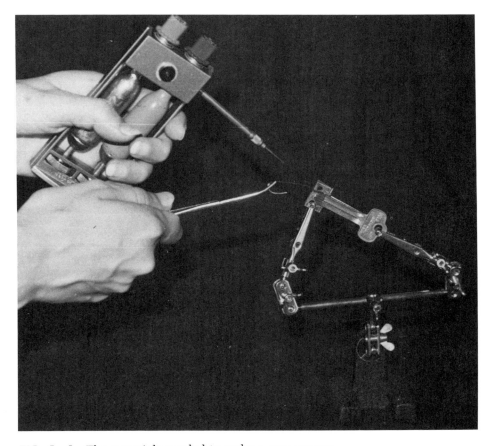

FIG. A—1   The materials needed to make a case popper.

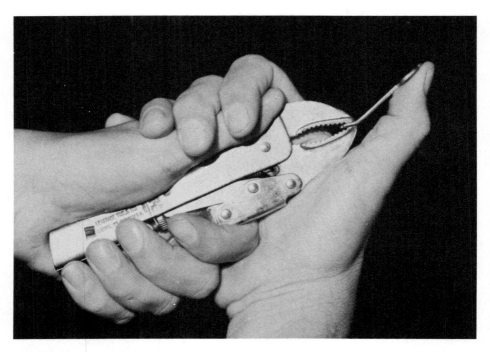

FIG. A—2 Carefully bend the two keys so that both have the same curve.

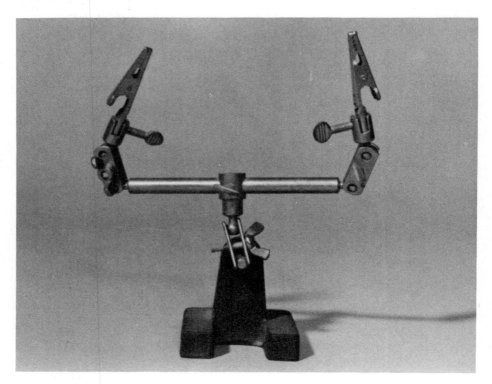

FIG. A—3 A helping hands tool can make building the case popper much easier.

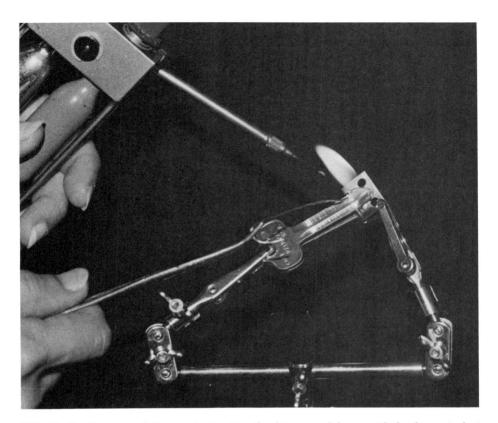

FIG. A—4 Very carefully apply heat to the hinge and key until the brass is hot enough to melt the solder.

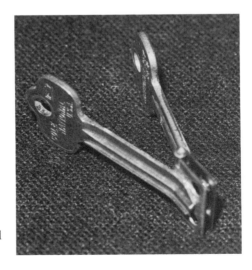

FIG. A—5 The finished "key to the Macintosh."

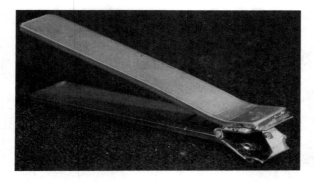

FIG. A—6 An alternate design, also using brass.

Place the hinge and one key in the helping hands. Now apply heat to them. A soldering gun or tool can be used, but it will have to be a powerful one. A torch with a small tip (small flame) works better. When the metal is hot, avert the flame and touch solder to the joint. The heat of the brass should melt the solder, not the heat of the flame. If you don't do it this way, your tool won't be very strong.

After you've finished one side, shut off the torch and let everything sit for a few minutes. It's all *very* hot. (If it's not, you haven't done it right.) Let it cool before you touch it.

Soldering the second side is a bit trickier. Again, your goal is to heat the brass of the hinge and key so that they melt the solder. When you do this, you might accidentally melt the solder on the first side. Careful use of the torch will help to reduce the chances of this. Try to not let the flame get near the first side as you're working on the second side.

Again let it cool before touching—and you're done.

Once you've assembled the case popper, learn to use it properly. This means, move slow and steady. Don't force the case apart. Start on one side, then move to the opposite side to complete the separation. The case is easier to separate if you start on the top. However, it is usually best to start on the bottom, because the first separation will require the most force, and if the case does receive some damage (it shouldn't if you're careful), it will be underneath the computer where it doesn't show.

Appendix B
Getting Inside the ImageWriter

There is rarely a need to take apart your ImageWriter. If the problem is a malfunction, first run the printer's self-test. To do this, start with the power off. Push down and hold the Form Feed button, then turn on the power. The self-test begins automatically, and continues to operate, testing the character set, until you shut off power again.

If this doesn't reveal the problem, go to Chapter 6 and the section on printers.

Only after you've done everything else possible should you attempt to take apart the ImageWriter. Even then, doing anything more than taking off the case can get you into trouble all too quickly. If you're one of those who will make use of this Appendix, removal of the case is where you should stop. Do not start yanking things out unless you know exactly what you're doing.

Unfortunately, there are times when taking apart the printer is the easiest solution to the problem. A good example of this is when something like a sheet of sticky labels gets jammed down inside. It's possible to fish out the jam with a paper clip, but the job is so much easier with the case out of the way.

Be sure that you pay attention to what you are doing. Move slowly, take notes and make sketches. Don't force anything. Whenever possible, label any parts you take off so you know where they go when you're putting the printer back together again.

The first thing to do is to completely disconnect the printer.

Two screws hold the top cover in place. One is easy to find (on the left side). The other is located beneath the control panel. Lift and unplug the control panel and look down inside. It should be fairly obvious which of the two screws inside holds the top cover in place. It is mounted through a plastic arm that is a part of the top cover. Carefully remove this screw. A

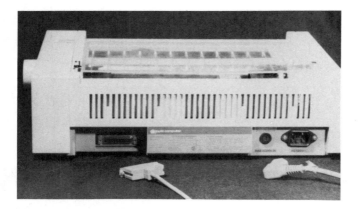

FIG. B—1 Disconnect the printer.

tweezer, needlenose pliers, or hemostat can help lift the screw out without dropping it.

The platen knob is held in place by a tight fit. Pull on it and it should come off easily. If it doesn't come, don't force it. Be patient.

The cover itself is held in place by four plastic catches in the back. These will break if you force them apart. Take your time. If the cover doesn't release quickly, a few gentle pushes around the catches will help.

One of the safety features of the ImageWriter (and many printers) is a lid sensor. This stops the printer from operating if the cover is lifted, making it difficult to get injured. The sensor has to be unplugged before you can remove the cover.

FIG. B—2 Remove the screw on the left side.

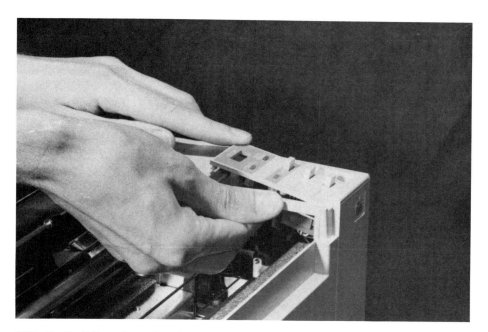

FIG. B—3 Lift and unplug the control panel.

FIG. B—4 Carefully remove the screw.

Chilton's Guide to Macintosh Repair and Maintenance
GETTING INSIDE THE IMAGEWRITER

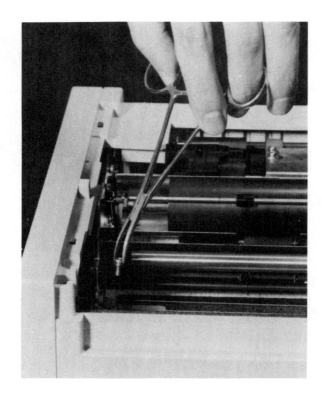

FIG. B—5 A tweezer, needlenose pliers, or hemostat will make removal and reinstallation of the screws easier.

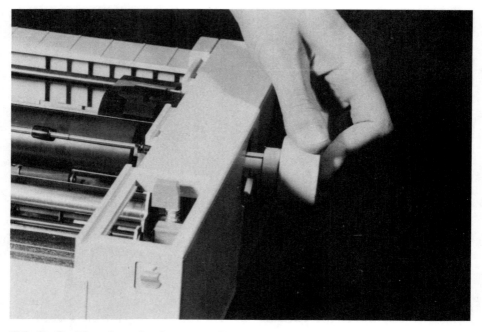

FIG. B—6 The platen knob comes off with a tug. Don't force it.

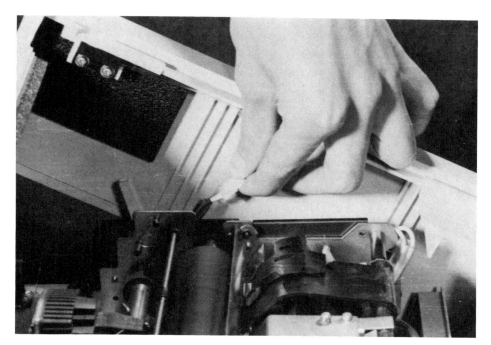

FIG. B—7 Unplugging the lid sensor.

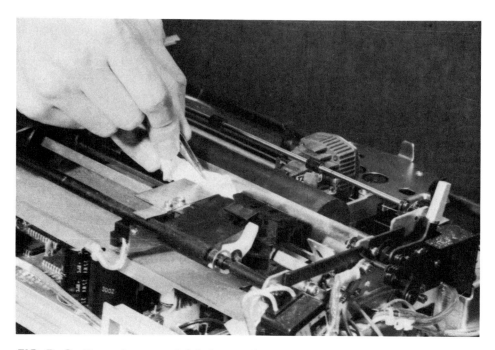

FIG. B—8 Removing a stuck label is much easier with everything out of the way.

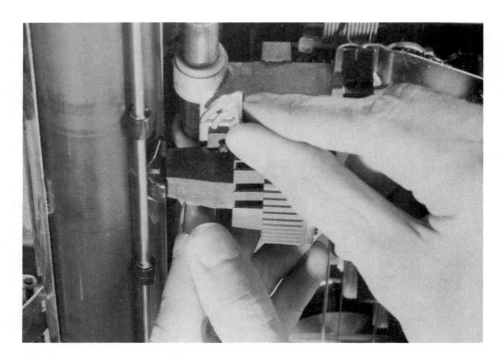

FIG. B—9 Moving the holding arms on the print head.

FIG. B—10 To remove the print head, first move the locking arms.

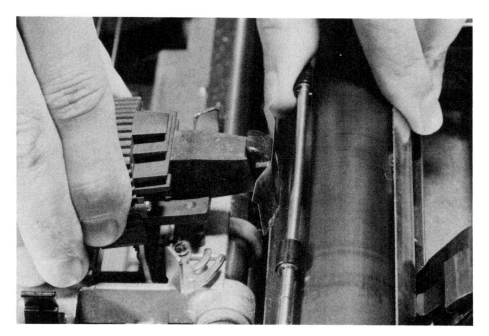

FIG. B—11 The print head will now lift out.

With the cover out of the way, it's much easier to get at problems, such as paper jams or crumpled labels. Cleaning the interior of the printer can also be done.

One final item can be removed. This is the print head. As tough as this piece is, sooner or later you may need to replace it. It is held in place by two metal arms beneath the head. Slide these forward. The head will still be tight, but it will lift out. Be careful not to damage it. Replacement of the new head is just the opposite. (Plug it in, and slide the arms back to lock the head in place.)

It's inadvisable to go any farther with the disassembly, however. There are tricky springs and other mechanisms inside. Some require special tools for reinstallation. Jobs that require further disassembly are best left to a professional, one who will guarantee that you'll end up with a working printer instead of a pile of loose nuts, bolts, and springs.

Appendix C
1 Meg+ RAM Upgrades

When the Macintosh was first introduced, it came with 128K of RAM. Apple promised a 512K version. Meanwhile, other companies developed ways to upgrade a 128K machine to the "Fat Mac."

Recently Apple announced that it would be releasing an upgraded ROM for the Macintosh that would allow it to access up to 4 megabytes of RAM. If everything goes according to schedule, this upgrade should be available by February 1986—before this book gets on the shelves.

Another alternative for Mac owners that does not involve changing the ROM chips is to upgrade the Macintosh to 1 or 1½ megabytes.

As with the upgrade from 128K to 512K described in Chapter 8, it is *not* advisable for the technically inexperienced owner to attempt the upgrade. There is a good chance of permanently damaging the main digital board of the computer. It's far better to let someone who knows how to do the job, and who will take responsibility, handle the upgrade.

You may save a little money by doing the job yourself, but not much. You probably won't save anything at all if you have to buy any special tools for the job.

If you decide to attempt it yourself, keep safety in mind at all times. For soldering, use *only* a soldering tool meant for the delicate digital circuits— and learn to be an expert on soldering *before* you begin. This is hardly the time to be experimenting.

As a general rule of thumb, upgrades beyond 512K require a cooling fan. It's possible to get by without the fan by using RAM chips that require less power to operate. (These chips are also more expensive.) One exception to this general rule is the 1.5-megabyte RAM upgrade from MacMemory, Inc., whose 1.5M upgrade uses only 1.3 watts of power.

Page through magazines that deal with the Macintosh for companies that provide RAM upgrades for the Macintosh. Before plunking down your money, there are a few precautions to keep in mind.

First, does the upgrade require changes or patches to the ROM chips? If it does, this company might find itself in legal difficulties. The architecture of the ROM chips is copyrighted by Apple. Anyone fiddling with that architecture may be in violation of copyright laws. And Apple has the reputation (and the justification) to go after those companies that commit the violation.

Second, be absolutely sure that the company doing the installation or selling the kit has a guarantee with the job and/or product. This guarantee should cover a period of *at least* 90 days. Generally, any problems will show up immediately. If it lasts past 90 days, it will probably continue to work just fine for years to come. (Obviously, if you buy a kit, the supplier can only guarantee the parts, and not the installation.)

Third, make sure that the upgrade or kit comes with all appropriate software. That extra memory won't do you much good if you can't get at it.

There are several ways to carry out a 1 megabyte or more upgrade. The following is the method used by MacMemory, Inc. Any kit you buy will come with complete instructions. The information below is more to acquaint you with the overall procedure and what is involved.

MAKING THE UPGRADE

Upgrades past 512K must start with a 512K machine. The easiest way to handle the upgrade is to ship either the computer or the main digital board to a company that can do the job and will guarantee it. To do this, find out what the company wants (the entire computer or just the main digital board).

If they want just the circuit board, open the case and remove the main digital board (as described in Chapter 5). MacMemory, Inc. makes this even easier by providing the tools needed to open the case and a shipping carton for the main board. The cost for this is an additional $12.50, payable in advance. If you have your own tools and a way to safely box up the board, there is no need to pay the extra cost.

Do be sure to package the board securely. Use anti-static packing material. Not just anything will work. It's a good investment to stop by an electronics supply shop for a sheet of anti-static material to wrap around the board. Then package everything up in a sturdy box.

Doing the job yourself is more difficult and time-consuming. Once again, if you aren't experienced with soldering and digital circuitry, you're much better off letting someone else do the job.

Remove the main digital board from the computer. Gather all the tools and parts you'll be needing for the job and get everything together in one spot. This spot should be roomy and static free. Preferably, the floor should not be carpeted as this can generate static. The board itself should rest on a static-free working surface that won't cause physical damage to the board.

There are two kinds of main digital board: revision C and revision D. If your computer came from Apple with 512K, you have revision D. If yours was a 128K board, whether upgraded to 512K or not, turn the board over and look for the identification mark. One of two revision numbers will be there, either 820-0086-C or 820-0086-D. It's that last letter you need.

You can also tell which board you have by looking at the coordinates of G and 13 on the component side of the board. The earlier revision C has two resistors here. The newer revision D has 16 holes in the configuration of a 16-pin IC. (In the 512K version, this spot will have a 74F253 chip installed.)

REVISION C

Find the CPU and the coordinate of E3. You'll see a line of seven holes. Next to this line will be a single hole. Clean out the solder from these holes.

Take an 8-pin socket header and clip off one of the two end pins. Now position the header over the seven holes and solder it into place. A single pin socket header goes into the single hole next to this strip.

Now turn the board over and locate the solder-side of the seven-pin strip. Pin 1 will be squarish. Very carefully, cut the trace between pins 1 and 2.

REVISION D

First, go to the G13 coordinate and remove the 74F253 chip, if one is installed. The holes must be clean, because a socket header, or a pair of 8-pin socket headers, will be installed.

If yours is a stock 512K board, you'll find three resistors near this spot, labeled R40, R41, and R42, and a capacitor marked C51. Remove the four components and clean the solder holes. Use a jumper wire to connect the two holes that held R42.

A 128K board will have ten holes (five pairs) near the socket header(s) and a jumper wire labeled "W1 128K Only." First, clean all the solder from the ten holes. Then remove the jumper and clean the holes. Finally, connect a jumper between the holes marked R42.

If you order your expansion board from MacMemory, you'll also have to make a few small revisions to that expansion board for D main boards.

On the new expansion board, near the cutout hole for the main board CPU, there is a 7-pin header and a 1-pin header. Neither is needed for a revision D Macintosh board. Either clip away all the pins, or completely remove the socket headers.

In the lower left corner of the expansion board is CN3. Two 8-pin socket headers are needed here. Solder both in place.

Finally, a jumper wire is needed between pin 7 (topmost, righthand side) of the resistor package at E3 on the Macintosh digital board and CN11 box on the far left side of the expansion board. Make the solder connection on the underside of the expansion board.

BOTH BOARDS

Find the coordinates E12 and E13 on the main board. Here you'll find two 74LS244 ICs. Remove both chips, clean the solder holes, and install a 10-pin socket header in each spot.

Find the coordinates F3 and F4. There are two chips here, with three solder holes between them. Clean out the two holes closest to Row G (bottom) of the board and solder in a 2-pin header.

Now find RP2 and RP3 (located at F4 and G4). Remove these resistor packages and replace them with 10-pin socket headers.

At the E7 coordinate above the CPU you'll see a line of eleven holes. Go to the hole at the farthest right and install a 1-pin header. Another 1-pin socket header gets installed in the hole at D3, just above the TSG label on the board.

Now thoroughly clean both boards of excess solder, flux, and so forth. Use a good-quality circuit board cleaner for this. Then visually inspect everything.

The only thing left is to plug in the expansion board, reassemble the computer, and test everything.

Tables and Charts

TABLE T–1. System Specs	
CPU	Motorola 68000 16-bit bus 32-bit internal 7.8 MHz
ROM	64K built-in
RAM	128K or 512K
CRT	Internal 4¾" × 7" (9" diagonal) 512 × 342 pixels (bit mapped) 60 lines per second
Input/output	2 serial (right rear) 1 external drive (center left rear) 1 mouse (left rear) 1 audio output (far right rear) 1 keyboard (right front)
Keyboard	58 key Onboard Intel 8021 processor
Mouse	Resolution 90 dots (pulses) per inch
Audio	3" speaker built in (auto disable with external plug) Ext., ⅛" phone plug (Radio Shack part #276-286) 1 volt peak-to-peak output
Clock/Calendar	Internal; uses Eveready #523 battery or equivalent
Main unit	9.7" × 10.9" × 13.5"; 16.5 lbs
Keyboard	13.2" × 5.8" × 1.5"; 2.5 lbs
Mouse	2.4" × 4.3" × 1.5"; 0.4 lbs
Operational temperature	50 to 104 F (10 to 40 C)
Storage temperature	−104 to 122 F (−40 to 50 C)
Operational humidity	5% to 90% relative
Operational altitude	Sea level to 15,000 feet

TABLE T–2. Diskette Specification Standards

Tracks (number)	80 per side
Track width	approx. 0.006 inch
Temperature (operation)	50 to 112 F 10 to 44 C
Temperature (storage)	−40 to 140 F −40 to 60 C
Humidity (operation) (storage)	20% to 80% 5% to 95%
Disk speed	390 to 605 rpm (slowest at outer edge)
Sector density per side	Outer 16 tracks: 12 sectors per track Next 16 tracks: 11 sectors per track Next 16 tracks: 10 sectors per track Next 16 tracks: 9 sectors per track Inner 16 tracks: 8 sectors per track
Total sectors	800 per side
Bytes per sector	512
Total bytes/side	409,600 per side

TABLE T–3.
Internal Drive Connector Pin Allocations
See Fig. 4–9

Pin	Use	Pin	Use
1	Ground	2	Phase 0
3	Ground	4	Phase 1
5	Ground	6	Phase 2
7	Ground	8	Phase 3
9	−12 VDC	10	Write Request
11	+5 VDC	12	Head Select
13	+12 VDC	14	Enable
15	+12 VDC	16	Read
17	+12 VDC	18	Write
19	+12 VDC	20	Motor

TABLE T–4. External Drive Pin Allocations
See Fig. 4–12

Pin	Use	Pin	Use
1	Ground		
2	Ground	11	Phase 0
3	Ground	12	Phase 1
4	Ground	13	Phase 2
5	−12 VDC	14	Phase 3
6	+5 VDC	15	Write Request
7	+12 VDC	16	Head Select
8	+12 VDC	17	Enable
9	No connection	18	Read
10	Motor	19	Write

TABLE T–5.
Power Supply Pin Allocations
See Fig. 6–11

Pin	Value	Pin	Value
1	Composite video	6	Ground
key	no pin	7	−12 VDC
2	Horizontal synch	8	Ground
3	Speaker	9	+12 VDC
4	Vertical synch	10	Battery
5	+5 VDC		

Note: Some sources list this as an 11-pin connector, with pin 2 being the key. Since there is no physical pin in this spot, I call it a 10-pin connector.

TABLE T—6. Main Board Resistance Check
(See Table 5—2 for example.)

Meter Used _____

Range Used _____

Part One—Entire System

Pin	Your Reading	Pin	Your Reading	Pin	Your Reading
1	_____	1	_____	1	_____
2	_____	2	_____	2	_____
3	_____	3	_____	3	_____
4	_____	4	_____	4	_____
5	_____	5	_____	5	_____
6	_____	6	_____	6	_____
7	_____	7	_____	7	_____
8	_____	8	_____	8	_____
9	_____	9	_____	9	_____
10	_____	10	_____	10	_____

Part Two—Drive Disconnected

Pin	Your Reading	Pin	Your Reading	Pin	Your Reading
1	_____	1	_____	1	_____
2	_____	2	_____	2	_____
3	_____	3	_____	3	_____
4	_____	4	_____	4	_____
5	_____	5	_____	5	_____
6	_____	6	_____	6	_____
7	_____	7	_____	7	_____
8	_____	8	_____	8	_____
9	_____	9	_____	9	_____
10	_____	10	_____	10	_____

Part Three—Main Digital Board Alone

Pin	Your Reading	Pin	Your Reading	Pin	Your Reading
1	_____	1	_____	1	_____
2	_____	2	_____	2	_____
3	_____	3	_____	3	_____
4	_____	4	_____	4	_____
5	_____	5	_____	5	_____
6	_____	6	_____	6	_____
7	_____	7	_____	7	_____
8	_____	8	_____	8	_____
9	_____	9	_____	9	_____
10	_____	10	_____	10	_____

Note: For these readings to be valid, they must be made while the board is known
to be good. Future readings will be compared to the original readings you get,
which means you must also use the same meter set to the same range. See
Chapter 5 for more details.

TABLE T–7. Keyboard Pins
See Fig. 6–6

Pin	Wire Color	Use
1	Black	Ground
2	Red	Keyboard clock
3	Green	Keyboard data
4	Yellow	+5 VDC

TABLE T–8.
Macintosh RS-422 Serial Port Pin Allocations
See Fig. 8–13

1	Ground	6	+12 VDC
2	+5 VDC	7	CTS/external clock
3	Ground	8	Receive data +
4	+ Transmit	9	Receive data −
5	− Transmit		

TABLE T–9.
Standard Parallel Pin Allocations
See Fig. 8–16

Pin	Use	Pin	Use
1	Strobe	10	Not used
2	Data bit 0	11	Busy
3	Data bit 1	12–15	Not used
4	Data bit 2	16–17	Ground
5	Data bit 3	18	Not used
6	Data bit 4	19–30	Ground
7	Data bit 5	31–32	Not used
8	Data bit 6	33	Ground
9	Data bit 7	34–36	Not used

TABLE T–10. Standard Serial (RS-232) Pin Allocations
See Fig. 8–15

Pin	Use	Pin	Use
1	Ground	6	Data set ready
2	Transmit data	7	Signal Ground
3	Receive data	8	Data carrier detect
4	Request to send	9–19	Not used
5	Clear to send	20	Data terminal ready

TABLE T–11. IEEE-488 Pin Allocations

Pin	Use	Pin	Use
1	Data bit 1	13	Data bit 5
2	Data bit 2	14	Data bit 6
3	Data bit 3	15	Data bit 7
4	Data bit 4	16	Data bit 8
5	End or Identify	17	Remote enable
6	Data available	18	Ground
7	Not ready	19	Ground
8	Data not accepted	20	Ground
9	Interface clear	21	Ground
10	Service request	22	Ground
11	Attention	23	Ground
12	Shield	24	Ground

IEEE-488 Bus Pinouts

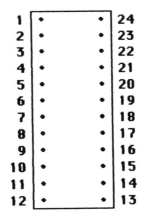

FIG. T–1 IEEE-488 pin allocations.

Mac-Mac Direct Connection
5-wires

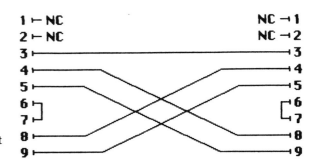

FIG. T–2 Direct connect between two RS-422 ports.

Chilton's Guide to Macintosh Repair and Maintenance
TABLES AND CHARTS

Mac-Mac Direct Connection
3-wires

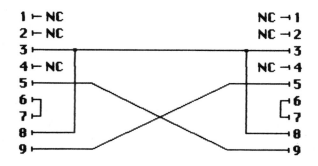

FIG. T–3 Alternate method for direct connect.

Mac to modem
4 wires

Mac DB-9　　　　　　　　**modem DB-25**

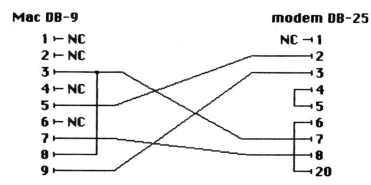

FIG. T–4 Simple Macintosh to modem connection.

Audio Output Jack

Tip - Audio out
Body - Ground

Output impedance: ≈47Ω　**FIG. T–5** Audio jack.

TABLE T–12. Mouse Wiring
See Fig. 6–7

1	Ground	6	No connection
2	+5 (filtered)	7	Button
3	Ground	8	Y2
4	X2	9	Y1
5	X1		

TABLE T–13.
Self-Test Sad Face Icon Error Codes

Code	Meaning
1	Malfunctioning ROM
2	Malfunctioning RAM
3	Malfunctioning RAM (write test)
4	Malfunctioning RAM (Mod3 test)
5	Malfunctioning RAM (location)

TABLE T–14. Self-Test RAM Location Chart

Subcode	Chip Location	Bit	Subcode	Chip Location	Bit
001	F5	0	0100	G5	8
002	F6	1	0200	G6	9
004	F7	2	0400	G7	10
008	F8	3	0800	G8	11
0010	F9	4	1000	G9	12
0020	F10	5	2000	G10	13
0040	F11	6	4000	G11	14
0080	F12	7	8000	G12	15

TABLE T–15. Self-Test—OF Exceptions Subcodes

Code	Meaning	Code	Meaning
0001	Bus error	0008	Trace
0002	Address error	0009	Line 1010 error
0003	Illegal instruction	0064	No start-up on disk
0004	Zero divide error	000A	Line 1111 error
0005	Check instruction	000B	Other
0006	Traps instruction	000C	Nothing
0007	Privilege violation	000D	Normal (interrupt)

Glossary

AC: Alternating current measured in cycles per second (cps) or hertz. The standard value coming through the wall outlet is 120 volts at 60 hertz. This voltage passes through a fuse or circuit breaker that can handle about 15 amps (check for yourself to know). Most computer power supplies can tolerate an AC value of between about 105 volts and 135 volts. The power supply changes this to the proper DC levels required by the computer.

Acoustic: Having to do with sound waves. For example, an acoustic modem sends and receives data as a series of audible beeps. (A direct-connected modem is better since it is not prone to interference or false signals due to room noise.)

Address: Where a particular piece of data or other information is found in the computer. See Chapter 5. Can also refer to the location of a set of instructions.

AppleTalk: A networking system, created by Apple and used for intercommunication between Macintoshes.

ASCII: This acronym stands for American Standard Code for Information Interchange. This code assigns binary (on/off) values to the 7-bit capability of the computer. The 8th bit is for special characters or characters with diacritical marks, to signal the end of the character, or for functions such as a parity bit to check for errors. ASCII is the standard code used to send data and other binary information, such as through a telephone modem.

Asynchronous: Often abbreviated "asynch." Refers to communications mode in which each character is balanced individually with timing or framing information (e.g., with a stop bit), as opposed to synchronous communication, in which a group of characters is given the timing.

Audio: A signal that can be heard, such as through a speaker.

Backup: A copy of a program or data diskette. Make them often to protect yourself.

Bank: The collection of memory modules that make up a block of RAM memory, often in increments of 16K or 64K, and usually done with 8 ICs.

BASIC: One of the most common first computer languages learned. Sometimes the BASIC used by a computer resides in the ROM memory. Other times it has to be loaded in from diskette or cassette tape. Although all BASICs are similar, they are not necessarily compatible with different computers.

Baud: Used to describe the speed of transmission. The signal is split into a certain number of parts per second. Thus 300 baud will send 300 units per second.

Generally each unit is a bit, so that 300 baud usually means that 300 bits per second are being sent.

Bit: A single pulse (on/off) of information used in binary code. The word "bit" is actually an abbreviation for "binary digit."

Boot: To load a program into the computer. The term comes from "bootstrap," which in turn comes from "lifting oneself by one's own bootstraps." It means that the computer is loading itself and is setting the computer to operate, without other operator intervention.

Buffer: A segment of memory, or a device, used to store data temporarily while the data is being transferred from one device to another. A common example is a printer buffer. This device stores the incoming data at full computer speed and sends it to the printer at a speed the printer can use (such as 40 characters per second, or about 300 baud).

Bug: An error in a program.

Bus: The pathway for the various signals used by the computer. Sometimes spelled "buss."

Byte: A collection of bits that makes up a character or other designation. Generally a byte is 8 data bits, the binary representation of a character.

Card: A circuit board.

Carrier: The reference signal used for the transmission or reception of data. The most common use with computers involves modem communications over phone lines. The modem monitors this signal to tell if the data is coming through. Generally, if the carrier isn't getting through, neither is the data.

Cassette: Either the device or the cartridge that is used in the device that stores and feeds information into the computer. The operation is very similar to that of an audio cassette. They are often used as a low-cost alternative to disk drives.

Catalog: A term used by Apple to describe the allocation track of a diskette. Stores the titles given to the files saved on the diskette and tells the computer and drives how to get to those files. The directory serves as a "table of contents" for the files saved on the diskette. The catalog sorts data that identifies the files by name, by size, by the kind of file stored (text file, binary file, etc.) and often the date the file was created. Information recorded on this track gives the computer the data it needs to find that file on the diskette.

Chip: Another name for an IC, or integrated circuit.

Circuit: A complete electronic path.

Circuit board: A collection of circuits on a sheet of plastic. The circuit board is usually made by chemically etching metal-coated phenolic plastic or fiberglass. Often the circuit boards in a computer are multilayered, which increases the efficiency but makes repairs to the tracings on the board difficult.

Common: The ground or return path used to make measurements with the multimeter. The black probe.

CP/M: Control Program for Microcomputers. One of the first, and still one of the most common, operating systems for microcomputers. Developed by Gary Kildall of Digital Research.

CPU: Central processing unit. Correctly refers to the main processing IC of the computer, but sometimes used to describe the entire main computer assembly.

CRC: Circle redundancy check. A means of checking the integrity of a data transfer.

CRT: Cathode ray tube. Basically a fancy name for a television or monitor screen tube.

Crystal: A small device located on various boards that vibrates at a particular frequency. One use is as a reference frequency for timing circuits.

Cylinder: A pair of tracks on opposite sides of a diskette. Used by the Macintosh and a few other computers to reduce wear on double-sided disk drives. The drive writes on the track on the first side, then on the track immediately on the other side of the diskette.

Daisy wheel: A circular printer element that holds all the characters to be printed (usually 96). The characters are on the end of thin arms all coming from the center, somewhat like the petals of a flower, which gives this print wheel its name.

Data: Information.

DC: Direct current, such as that provided by the power supply. (Also found in batteries.)

Debug: To rid a program of errors, or bugs.

Default: An assumption the computer makes when no other parameters are specified. For example, if you type the command for the directory or catalog without specifying the drive to search, the computer automatically goes to the default drive (normally the last one selected) and assumes that this is what you want. The term is used in software to describe any action the computer or program takes on its own with imbedded values.

Density: The amount of information that can be packed into a given area on a diskette. Diskettes are usually rated as being single density, double density, or quad density.

Directory: The allocation track on a diskette. See *catalog*.

Diskette: The magnetically coated media used most often in computers for the storage of data.

DOS: Disk operating system. The set of commands that allows the computer to access the data on the diskettes. For the Macintosh, this is more correctly called the system file.

Drive: The device used to read and write on diskettes. If the drive is a "fixed" drive, it is commonly called a hard drive or "Winchester drive." The drive can also be electronic, using RAM instead of the magnetic media.

Dvorak: A relatively new keyboard layout that increases efficiency and typing speed. Named after its inventor, August Dvorak.

Edit: To make a change or modification in data.

Emulate: A fancy word for "pretend to be." Used to describe a device that is designed to make the computer *seem* to operate like another computer or terminal.

Execute: To start a program or instruction set.

FAT: Files Allocation Table. An area on the diskette used to allocate space for files. The information included in the table indicates which sectors on the diskette are free and which are used.

Fat Mac: A Macintosh computer with 512K RAM built in.

FCC: Federal Communications Commission. Regulates the kind and amount of radio frequencies that can be emitted by computers and computer devices.

Ferric oxide: The iron substance most often used as the magnetic medium on diskettes (Fe_2O_3). Essentially it is nothing more than rusted iron.

File: Any collection of information saved on a diskette. The file can be data, a program to run, or both.

Finder: A program used by the Macintosh that allows you to manipulate files and run other programs.

Firmware: The ROM of the computer.

Flippy: A diskette with notches and index holes cut into both sides, allowing the diskette to be used on both sides by a single-sided drive (by flipping the diskette over). Not possible with the Macintosh.

Font: One of a number of lettering styles. Many matrix printers are capable of using a variety of print styles, changeable through software.

Footprint: The amount of room the computer equipment takes up on the work table.

Format: A command within DOS that assigns various tracks and sectors to new diskettes. Also called "initializing." Also, a particular manner in which something is laid out, such as in a program.

Ground: The common or return side of a circuit. (See *common*.)

Handshake: When two devices "talk" to each other to determine the rate of data transfer. This is very important when one device is slower than another—such as a printer and computer. In a sense, the printer tells the computer to stop transmitting until the printer catches up again.

Hardware: The computer and computer devices.

Head: The read/write head of the disk drive.

Hertz (Hz): A measure of frequency. One cycle per second (cps). Frequency is also measured in units such as kilohertz (KHz—thousands of cycles per second) and megahertz (MHz—millions of cycles per second).

IC: Integrated circuit. This is a package of electronics, often encased in black plastic, with pins coming from the bottom. Pin 1 is the first pin on the right on the side with the notch or other marking.

Icon: A picture that represents something. With the Macintosh, icons are used both externally (to label the ports for example) and within many programs.

Index hole: Small holes on a diskette near the hub access hole, used by some computers to find the beginning of a sector. Not used by all computers.

Initialize: Means the same as "format" when it comes to diskettes. This routine sets up the diskette into the proper number and location of tracks and sectors so the Macintosh can use it.

Interface: A fancy term for "connect." Used to describe any connection from hardware to hardware, from hardware to software, or even from hardware and/or software to user.

I/O: Input/output. Where data enters or leaves the computer.

K: With computers, usually used to describe an amount of memory. Normally "K" denotes 1000 (such as in kilohertz above). Due to the electronics involved, 1K of memory is actually 1024 bytes; 64K is actually 65,536 bytes.

Keyboard: Primary means of manual input to a computer.

LED: Light emitting diode, such as those used in the drives to sense disk insertion or write protect.

Light pen: An instrument designed to read areas on the screen by pointing at them. Used to input data to the computer in a manner similar to that of a mouse (see *mouse*) in addition to or instead of a keyboard.

Matrix: A pattern of dots, in computer printers used to make up letters, numbers, and other symbols.

Microfloppy: Floppies that are less than 3½" in diameter. The three main types are from designs developed by Sony, Hitachi/Maxell, and Tabor.

Minifloppy: Still another name for a diskette. Describes a 5¼" floppy.

Modem: A device for transmitting data over telephone lines. The name means "modulate-demodulate."

Monitor: A television-like device to display characters and other symbols. Also called a display, CRT, or VDU.

Mouse: A handheld input device moved across the surface of a CRT. It is used to input data to the computer and to get quickly from one spot on the screen to another.

MS-DOS: A disk operating system developed by Microsoft, and one of the most popular in use. Called PC-DOS when used in the IBM PC.

Multimeter: A device to measure volts and ohms across a variety of ranges. Often called a VOM.

Nanosecond: A unit of time used to describe the operating speed of computers, particularly RAM chips. 1 nanosecond equals 1 billionth of a second. A 150 ns RAM chip, then, has an operating speed of 150 billionths of a second (or .15 millionths of a second).

Network: Two or more computers connected together, usually to share information or a device. For example, two computers can be networked so that both use a single hard drive.

Null modem: Direct writing two computers for communication.

Ohm: Unit of measurement of resistance.

Operating system: DOS, CP/M, or some other system that allows the computer to operate.

Parallel: A means of data transfer with the information being sent a byte at a time. (See also *serial.*)

Parity: A means of error checking. Parity checking can be even, odd, or none. Even parity checking means that the number of 1 bits (on) must be even in the byte. Odd parity means that the number of 1 bits in a byte must be odd. *None* means no parity checking is done.

PET: Polyethylene terephtalate, the generic name of the material used to make diskettes. Common trademark name is "Mylar" (owned by Dupont).

Pixel: Shortened form of "picture element," or a single dot on the screen. Used to describe the clarity or resolution of a monitor.

Platen: The rubber roller of the printer.

Port: A place where cables are connected to the computer or other device. Sometimes called an interface.

Program: A set of instructions the computer can understand and act upon to perform some useful (or useless) task.

Queue: Data waiting to be processed. For example, text being held in a buffer waiting to be printed. Pronounced "cue."

QWERTY: Describes a standard typewriter keyboard (based on the placement of the letters at the upper left of the keyboard).

Resolution: The clarity of the image on the screen. Sometimes used to describe printer image quality.

Sector: An area on the track of the diskette assigned to hold a certain amount of information. The amount of data held per sector depends on the computer and DOS being used.

Serial: A means of data transfer in which information is handled a bit (or pulse) at a time, with each bit following the others.

Soft sector: A method of setting up a diskette so that data is written first to a sector whose position is determined by a code stored on disk.

Software: Computer programs, usually on diskette.

Source: Where a signal originates.

Spindle: The device in the disk drives that is inserted into the center hole and causes the diskette to spin.

Spooler: A kind of printer buffer.

Stepper motor: Used to move the read/write heads across the surface of the diskette.

Stop bit: Signals the end of a byte in asynchronous communication.

Switching power supply: A kind of power supply often used in microcomputers. Power levels are determined by the rapid switching on and off of regulators, transistors, and other digital components.

System board: The main circuit board of the computer. Sometimes called the "motherboard." (Correctly, motherboard applies only to Apple computers.) Also called the main board.

Target: Where a signal is to terminate. For example, if you are copying a file, the target is the diskette on which the file is to be copied.

Terminal: In a computer system, a device through which data can be entered or retrieved. Can also be the end point of an electrical connection. Sometimes used to describe a monitor (i.e., video terminal).

Torx: A special kind of screw used to hold the Macintosh together. The 6 points and straight sides provide superior anti-stripping capabilities.

Track: One of the concentric rings on a diskette.

TVI: Television interference. Computers and some computer devices emit radio frequencies that can cause interference of normal television operation.

VOM: Volt-ohm-milliammeter. Commonly called a multimeter.

Write/protect: A hole and sliding cover formed into the diskette case allows a sensor in the drive to activate the recording head. With the cover back and the hole open, the recording head is disabled, making recording onto the diskette impossible (hopefully).

Index

Page numbers in *italic* indicate illustrations;
page numbers followed by *t* indicate tables.